THE

REVELATION

OF

CHOICE

THE
REVELATION
OF
CHOICE

REVELATIONS
THAT WILL INSURE
YOUR HAPPINESS
AND SUCCESS

BERNIE HESTER JR.

PALMETTO
PUBLISHING
Charleston, SC
www.PalmettoPublishing.com

Paperback ISBN: 979-8-8229-3887-8

DEDICATION

To all who seek success. May we all receive the miracle of love and the miracles of life awaiting us.

To my miracles. Teachers: Mary Frances Parker, Latin; Sam Litchfield, Geometry; and Virginia von Lehe, English.

To my mentor. W.C. Carter, the man who saw in me the spark of success and made it a reality.

To my miracles. My children: Tammy, Bernie, and Sharon.

To the love that was my greatest miracle: Frances.

A special mention: Ryan Hester, a perfect example of the law of miracles.

TABLE OF CONTENTS

PREFACE

When I first entered my life, I thought I was in a beautiful garden. I could hear the vibrations of the universe. To this day I can recall the bright colors of the flowers and the freshness of life. There was excitement and a sense of wonderment that slowly began to fade away as my life began to flow.

The forming of my life became more about conforming to the thoughts and needs of those around me. Something inside me felt constrained and unnatural. Instead of becoming myself, I was becoming the person that those around me wanted me to be.

There were more questions than answers. Why was there evil? Why did God allow suffering? What was original sin? Why did God condemn us? Why was there a hell? Why do we have to die? Why does God depend on humans to save and control my life? Who are we and why are we here? What is success in my life? How can I be the best that I can be? Which decisions in my life did I make which empowered me to become the person I wanted to be? Which decisions made my life a struggle and forced me into becoming less than the person I wanted to be? What are my discoveries? What has been revealed to me? A life is a life well lived when these questions are answered.

DISCLAIMER

This book is based entirely on my life experiences. It is about my personal discoveries on how to be a success as they were revealed to me. This is my book of revelations. Nothing in this book is based on research and documentation. It is all about reality. My success is the result of my personal discoveries. It is all about the true nature of creation and the formation of the universe.

INTRODUCTION

Why is it that we are, from birth, persuaded to believe that our life will be a painful, almost unbearable, existence? Why is that life, for most of us, ends up being nothing more than an ever-present feeling that unknown forces or others around us have used and depleted us. Is it that once our life is over, we often wonder how it all ended up with no clear meaning? An alarming number of us live no lives of our own and this is a tragedy. Can this be avoided?

There are unchangeable laws which make up the universe and form creation. We have the choice to use them or we can choose to ignore them. Those who accept them will become a success. These choices belong to each of us from the time we enter life. These laws will not change. They are unalterable laws that we must freely choose to follow. These laws enable each of us to live a good life. We have the freedom of choice: to choose success. We are at a critical point in our understanding of the power of choices. We have the gift of choice with no penalties for making incorrect choices. The universe was designed with no controls other than the laws of creation. These laws are very few and easy to understand.

If you make the choice to read this book and read each page carefully, taking the time to separate the known from the unknown, you will discover the secret of living the life you were created to live. We must choose these laws if we are to achieve happiness and fulfillment in our lives.

This book will offer you insights into the unlimited consequences of choices. You will be the beneficiary of the discoveries and truths I have found over the decades of my life with countless thousands of hours doing my own thinking. I have almost total recall of every aspect of my life from the time I became aware of life. At first I thought that life was random and accessible only to a selected few. An elite number of us would be the chosen ones. But who does the choosing?

The chosen ones, you will discover, are no more than myths and illusions. You will see in real time the devastating outcome of making incorrect choices and why it is that our choices are so powerful. Are we here on Earth as the chosen ones or among the ones given no choice? Find out why this might be, and if so, why. Not only why, but also how this came to be. We will seek answers together, exploring every aspect of choice and choices. Life flows through all of us with the same force. This force is the freedom of spirit we aspire to live within each day of our lives. We are equal in the creative processes, so then why not equal in choices?

You will fully understand choice and the nature of choices. This will be your gift. There is one outcome you can be sure of: you will discover the POWER OF CHOICE. You will have the freedom to choose or not to choose this power. You will, once you have read this book, always think carefully before you make future choices. If you choose to accept this new revelation, you will remove all the fear and anxiety from your life and experience excitement and energy once again in your essence.

The understanding of correct choices will be worth your time and effort. This knowledge will be yours any time you choose to access it. You will find it to be an uncomplicated pathway that will change your life. Life is not complicated. Creation is not complicated. Once you or I choose to accept this truth, our unique creation will be revealed, and we will experience ever upward levels of awareness. This is the creative design for each of us as creation continues on its journey to perfection. You and your life will be changed, and it will be easy to see and feel all the newfound beliefs and changes these correct choices have released back into your life once again. This is a process we all can begin in this moment. You will discover how to achieve success and find the meaning of your life.

We are in the beginnings of our creation. Success as we know it may not be possible. We must discover the universe within each of us or choose to drift into nothingness. Success is easy to achieve in a universe based upon reality. All this and more is yours to choose.

CHAPTER 1:
UNDERSTANDING SUCCESS AS A CHOICE

In this chapter it will be revealed how your personal choices can improve you and your place in life and at the same time ensure your success. It is your guide on how to improve yourself in the now. If you follow this plan, you will begin to see the results at once. The truth is that you do not have the power to change the universe, but you have the unlimited power to control the you that you can be and therefore you can change yourself. You will be able to use this power to fulfill your potential to the maximum, limited only by your purpose for existing. You will reach the level of perfection given to you at birth. This is your guarantee: you can change yourself.

You will reach your maximum level of success and happiness to only be exceeded during your next upward level in your existence. Once you become the unique you that you were created to be, you will have achieved your success by finding your achievable reality. Your life is yours to create once you decide to design it and then make the choice to begin the process. The reality is that you have this inner power ; limited only by your inborn potential. The first step in changing is to accept that a change is needed. We all have the power to choose this new revelation.

Do we have choices or is everything predetermined by fate? We will not be able to understand choice until we fully understand and accept the universal laws of creation. These laws were fashioned by our Creator. This means that they cannot be changed, redesigned, or amended in any form, nor need they be. As you read each page, you will see how this is all about you and your success. There are limited dimensions, but once you access all of them you will see your success materialize right before your eyes.

As you read each chapter, it will be revealed to you the importance of your soul. The conditions we find ourselves now living in are not as they were intended to be. Success is not success unless and until we all learn to love ourselves and then everyone around us. There are revelations to be discovered which will ensure your success, but it may not be the kind of success you now expect: illusionary success. Success as defined under the law of limited expectations is the only success that we all can reach.

The success that illusions and myths have created it to be is not attainable. It is the same with our self-created alternate realities. Before we can make any sense of who we are and have the potential to become, the entire structure of the universe we now live in must be exposed for the illusion it is, and the illusion of success that we now live in must be exposed for the illusion it is. We will do this, beginning now. Come with me and together we will search for both success and happiness. The answers are inside all of us. Our individual success is within us already. Our individual success is certain if we follow all the laws of success. This book is a summary of the revelations of the universe and laws of success that are in all of us.

There are laws which will guarantee you the success in your life you were created to experience. Master these simple laws. If you do, you will never need to read another book on how to become a success again.

The Design of the Universe

This never-changing design was the Creator's choice; therefore, it will never be a choice that we can change. We have the gift to make choices, but all our choices are limited by our awareness levels and begin inside our created selves. This may be better understood in this way: we have choices, but they may not be the correct choices. When we make incorrect choices, we no longer have access to creation and the creative processes. Incorrect choices create illusions and myths and are destructive. At the very minimum, they remove us from our own life, the life we have the potential to experience.

From the time we make our first incorrect choices, our lives begin to lose focus and meaning. This concept may be confusing to you. But the explanation is that we are life, and our Creator is life. The result is that our Creator is the source of the person we can choose to be. This is the same process through which all living things can have access to choose once they are elevated to the required awareness level. All who achieve success in life understand their freedom to choose. This is the beginning of your success; you can begin now because you are the decider in your existence.

As we move up in our creation, the more choices we will have, but we must always be aware of this truth: our choices cannot change or enhance the laws of creation as designed by our Creator. When the choices we make are incorrect, they create illusions and myths, thereby permanently or temporarily removing us from our intended place in creation. Choices are the catalysts in the creative processes. Incorrect choices remove us from our intended existence because choice is the beginning of all things in creation. Intelligence alone does not make choices correct ones; if a choice is to be correct, all the laws of creation must be included. You will either understand and choose to accept this or choose to reject this and thereby halt your participation in your unique existence in creation. Understanding this truth will make every choice you make a correct choice, thereby supporting your existence. Your focus will be overpowering. So overpowering that nothing can stand in your way. This means that you will become a more perfect soul; nothing can take this away. This is your guarantee.

The truth is that our Creator allows no one but each of us individually to make choices for ourselves, that is, unless we make the incorrect choice to allow others to choose for us. We are allowed to choose not to accept this truth, but even if we do, creation will continue. This is because choices are all included in the flow of creation. Choices are unavoidable. Making no choice is in itself a choice.

Creation is not subject to our will or tries to control it. If this were true, we would thereby become the creators. We cannot create so we try to control creation through force, regulations, lies, and false illusions, the result being that we create an alternate universe filled with our delusions of power, domination, and control. We are so obsessed with being in control that we are willing to deceive our own selves. We are allowed the choice of self-deception. This is all included in the law of miracles. But even with the law of miracles to protect us, it certainly makes our individual choices in our daily living even more important. So, it will be life-changing once we become determined to make the correct choices. It will be that simple. All we need to do is begin the process now. All choices made by each of us which do not follow, and therefore are in denial of, our Creator's choices are ineffective.

We personify control as evil. But evil is not an entity. We created evil as our justification of our need to control. Incorrect choices cannot exist in the universe, only in a false, meaningless universe, filled with unlimited forms of mind control and gaslighting. Your success requires that you master the simplicity of the universe and transform your life to follow these truths in your daily existence. But first you must stop deceiving yourself. The only control we have is over ourselves. We also do not have the awareness levels to create anyone or anything other than ourselves.

The deceptions of the last twenty thousand years will be almost impossible to overcome. But if you persevere and be patient, all will be revealed. One fact is certain: you can survive it all.

It is obvious that we all want to become a success. But what is success if it must be reached through the pain and suffering of ourselves or others? What is life if it is lived in a false universe created by others at the expense of our eternal selves? First, we must understand universal laws; only then will we know and experience our unique success.

We must remove mysticism, magical thinking, and fear from our life. We then must replace it all with this truth: the miracles we look for are within our being. Prepare to be amazed when you allow them to be revealed. Everything comes from the center. This is true for the universe and true for your success. Your success comes from your heart, so you will find it nowhere else. Success, in a sense, is obtaining your heart's desire.

Success and happiness, at this time, is restricted to those in power and control. We must first return our species to our known reality once again. Success is not serving others. Success may be defined as serving our purpose. Finding our purpose will give our lives meaning. Understanding where we are and beginning the process to become who we are created to be will, in the end, enable each of us to achieve success.

We believe that our self-created reality is all there is. We lose our souls when we allow ourselves to accept this explanation of our reality. Our success is based upon the discovery of self. The truth is that we all have within our beings the ability to succeed. But if we are to advance ourselves, it is absolutely essential that we return to our natural existence. But to do this requires a self-awareness that we can choose to reach. The good news is that you can begin this process now; no need to wait. When the process is complete, it may well be that our success will be measured by how well we understand our place in the universe. We are the chosen, but do we choose to accept this truth.

We each are given life but to what end? There can be no assurance of happiness or success. It is our choice. Our greatest challenge is our self-control. Our Creator knew this. This is why our Creator made our success our choice.

CHAPTER 2:
ANCIENT HUMANS

This is an overview rather than an in-depth attempt at contrasting or disproving all the mystical and illusionary speculations on the origins of our species. All theories are mentioned, religious beliefs, scientific interpretations, alien visitations, and mutations. Most will be outside the laws of creation and thereby impossible to be a reality. The continuous streaming of illusions and myths throughout our recorded history has served to deny and suppress our origins.

Time as we know it may not be. There is no proof that time exists at all. Time measurements are not useful in a universe which was and is. Your time is now.

According to recorded history, from approximately five thousand five hundred years ago, going all the way back hundreds of thousands of years, humans slowly formed. There are no records confirming how or when we began. I use the term ancient humans because there is no link marking the transition from primitive humans to ancient humans. It is all the more baffling because there are so many opinions, theories, beliefs, and myths speculating on how we have originated and how we evolved to become modern humans. There is only one known source. This source is our Creator; therefore, our emergence was structured by the laws of creation. Other than the Creator, all in creation have limited choices. To know this is the beginning of wisdom. We all have the awareness to choose wisdom.

Accepting the unknown and telling it as factual may in the end be the fall of modern humans. Unfortunately, mathematics, science, history, and religions have all told the unknowns as knowns. There are no records, either written or included in all of our sciences, mathematics, histories, or religions, which recognize choices as being central in creation. I am the first to find choice as the central component in creation. If this revelation proves to be true, I will be in a good place, for my discovery will reveal to you your true identity and will change your life in the now. Living the life you were born to live is the true definition of your success.

The power of choices has been known but denied from the event of modern humans even up to now. The future is decided by the choices made in the now. We cannot change the past, but we can decide who we will become in the future. In creation, the future is in the now and not in some imaginary place in time.

It has always been a reality that we have the power to make correct choices. We have the awareness, but we are free to choose not to accept this truth. The Creator designed it this way. Because it was the Creator's design, we will never be denied the power of our limited self-choices as a central law of our existence in creation. We must always continue to re-mind ourselves that our individual creation is self-limiting; therefore, our choices are limited to our own existence and, as a result, we are unable to make choices for others.

Our Creator designed creation this way. Indeed, we can try to have it our own way through the use of control. But in the end, we will not be able to succeed. It is and always will be our choice to remain in creation or choose to become part of lost illusions and nothingness. If we choose illusions, our souls may never advance to the next higher level of aware-ness. Reality has always been the same. We live in it, but we have only the ability to access the surface of universal reality. We have no time to waste by creating our own unworkable false ones.

There is excitement in discovering the laws of creation. For those who have already made this discovery, this feeling is not new. This excitement is everywhere in their daily existence. If only every one of us would stop wanting to control how everyone else lives their lives, our awareness would suddenly rise to even higher and higher levels. This is our challenge, the elimination of control. The revelation is: you can choose your success.

Who are we and why? There are many mythical theories. So many fabrications with no substance. The general consensus is that any theory or explanation will work as long as everyone accepts it or if those in control force everyone to believe it to be true and binding. As we continue our urge to control, think about this, and question why this is and then why this can be and is happening. Control has become our self-created God. This is to say that in reality we worship control.

Primitive humans, according to all speculations and theories, have been around for millions, if not billions, of years. There is no knowledge of the time period when primitive humans began fading away and then to morph into ancient humans and their higher level of awareness. The general agreement is that this process began millions of years ago. The precise time is not important. But the cosmic impact would be that our species would never be the same again. We either go higher in creation or we cease to be in creation as we were designed when our entity was formed. Discover your purpose and you will then be able to achieve your success.

Primitive humans did not use words or languages to survive. They had limited awareness. The choices were: fight or flight. Even these choices were more of a reflex than a conscious decision. It is now clear that our species, during this time, changed in our awareness levels and in countless other ways. As a result of the sudden appearance of ancient humans, our species became an enigma. The full impact of this event has not been figured out even up to now. Did we change or were we subject to as of yet unknown forces? It must be that all this is within our Creator's laws of creation. If this is correct, then we will eventually even more fully understand why. Accept the limitations of creation and you will begin the process of your success and happiness.

How does this affect you? It clearly shows the reality that you cannot change the past or remove thousands and millions of years of control and suppression of reality. The meaning for you is that you can remove control in your life in this moment in time, in the now. You have control over your existence. You are the deciding factor. Become the master of your universe. In the end we have the potential to become the chosen ones. But there is no predetermination, only choice. We have the power and awareness, but we must remove the fears that blind us. There is, within each of us, the entire universe just waiting to be experienced. It must be admitted that we may not be eternal in our present form. Modern humans and ancient humans can no longer exist together; only one form can survive. Now is the time for each of us to make a choice. There is no success, and therefore no happiness, in choosing to remain a slave to control, no matter the circumstances or illusions we conjure up in explaining our failings.

CHAPTER 3:
MODERN HUMANS

The genesis of the emergence of modern humans has stimulated more controversy than any event in our brief history on this earth. At no time in our brief existence have so many universal laws been put aside. Modern humans threaten to alter our place in creation. This chapter will provide you with discoveries which may be utilized in your quest to maximize your life and make your life a journey worth taking.

A new species suddenly emerged through a mutation or other processes not yet understood. First there were primitive humans, then, in an instant, they were no more. This sudden transformation resulted in the appearance of modern humans but with no known explanations of how this transformation of our species suddenly emerged. There are numerous claims but no unquestionable explanations. It seems to be, at this time, more like a cosmic conflict. An epic struggle between two dissimilar forms to dominate each other. The result being that one must replace the other one, the two must merge, or that our species risks becoming extinct.

Modern humans must accept and conform to the laws of creation. But will they choose to? We have created our own alternate universe, dressed it up in myths and illusions. We will go into a rage and destroy anyone daring to question our exaggerated self-importance. There are those who control our perceptions of reality. They hold the key to an alternate universe. They separate those who have from the have nots and the chosen from the unchosen. It is as if modern humans have taken over control of primitive humans with the intent of using them as a host or as a means of survival or slave labor, thereby taking away from us all our self-choices, in order to use and hold on to their control with illusions and myths. This concept is frightening. It is the use of control to twist reality and defy creation. If this is true, then we must refuse to accept modern human's false realities and choose our own way out.

Modern human's sudden emergence could be a mutation event. If this is true, then there are only three outcomes: the mutants spread among the population and replace the older species, both species coexist, or the mutants cease to be. Our species must reclaim our own choices. We must understand that we cannot be controlled: there is no control. Control is an illusion. Denial does not validate the illusion of control. Denial is a form of self-deception. It has been said that the greatest lie we will ever tell is the lie we tell ourselves. Modern humans have been telling themselves these lies from the beginning. The good news is that creation was designed for the survival of primitive humans. There are more primitive humans than modern humans. So, we each have the power of choice to reclaim our place in creation.

As things now stand, primitive humans do not visualize their own power of choice. All of us continue to exist within universal laws. We are absolutely free to reject control. Modern humans are only indoctrinating and gaslighting us to make us afraid so we will believe we do not deserve to make our own choices. The life we once experienced did not suddenly end. Modern humans chose to control us, and this may prove to be a nonreversible, incorrect choice. But the reality is that under the laws of creation, modern humans are part of the divine plan for our species. But the outcome of the emergence of modern humans threatens to alter our place in the universe. The choice is for all of us to make. But first we must reclaim ourselves.

Modern humans are new arrivals with origins unknown. Nevertheless, modern humans must change and adapt to the unchangeable laws of the universe. There are any number of speculations on the origins of modern humans: mutations, evolution, alien invasion, new creations, or even that modern humans are gods, but no matter the source, modern humans cannot be exempted from or in control of the creative laws and processes. The assumption that modern humans are the center of creation is based upon illusions and myths they have created during their short existence, exemplified by denying reality, and using the illusion of control. As a result, the never-ending attempts to control condemns all of us to a universe of illusions. Only now it is revealed to each of us that there is a way to reverse all uses of control. We must rediscover our place in creation. We can begin this process by rediscovering ourselves.

What are modern humans' contributions? How much progress have they made? What have they changed? We now have the most advanced weapons, and we continue to find ways to create more. Yet there continues to be widespread oppression and irrational rage, leading to irrational behavior. If only our species will once again begin making correct choices, hunger and poverty would cease to exist. At this moment in time, far too many of our species are living without proper nourishment, in general poverty, and as servants. We, as a species, have all we need to live a good life, but a relative few claim it all for themselves, thereby enslaving the many by framing themselves to be the chosen ones.

All that modern humans have created are illusions and myths under the false claim that without their control, the universe will cease to be and that all our advancements would never have occurred. Any rational assessment of the past six thousand years of modern humans' progress and achievements will expose this illusion and all the myths created to support this alternate reality. The reality is they have created nothing except their own version of life and creation, and as a result of the choice to be in control, we are going to choose to return to nothingness. This will be our downfall. Unless we rediscover who we are and were created to become, our short-lived existence will consist of sound and fabrications ending in nothing. It seems to be that we are allowed to make these incorrect choices because our universal laws allow us to temporarily exist. But only if we choose this outcome. The incorrect choice of control will be our irrational choice if we choose it. It is important to note that choice will always be the portal to perfection. The destruction of self occurs when your choices are taken away from you. Without yourself, your soul, there can be no success.

The brief history of modern humans is proof of the results of making incorrect choices. We rationalize our need to control by, in effect, blaming it on outside circumstances. That we are both the reason for the need of control and reason for creation is a distorted illusionary myth, supported by a contorted illusion of reality. Are we so lacking in the ability to reason, or could it be that we are delusional? Just because we can choose this illusion does not make it reality based. The universe is efficient. We must accept it as our Creator formed it. Are we ready to receive this gift, the gift of choice or not yet, at our needed place of awareness? Is a modern mutation manipulating us to be unable to accept our Creator and the laws of creation? Ancient humans may be more in harmony with creation than modern humans. All evidence seems to be that we are. We must begin making our own choices once again. This is the first choice that we have to make. In the now is the time to choose creation.

We can choose to accept the laws of creation, but will we or can we? Are modern humans mutations? No matter the source or the reasons, our species will not remain in creation if we continue to choose the illusion of control. This is the reason for all our sufferings and frustration: our choice to be in control. It is worth mentioning that modern humans exhibit many symptoms of a narcissistic personality. Are we unwilling victims or suffering from our own coping mechanisms? This is something to consider because it would explain how we came to be this way.

All indications are that we became this way after the sudden appearance of modern humans. We are being gaslighted and devalued, and as a result, we feel unloved and unable to see ourselves as we really are. How do we free ourselves from these narcissistic controllers? We must choose to remove them from our lives. Once these illusions are removed, our species will be able to remove all our sufferings and frustrations. If we do, our species will survive and once again experience the love and fulfillment we were created to experience.

It is plausible that our species is doing this to our own selves, but then if not us, what is the source? We will never evolve as our Creator designed our species to until we first admit that we cannot be designers. It is certain that we have the power to remove incorrect choices within our control. But the question is: will we remain in creation? If not, then what is our place in creation at this moment in time? If we exist only to enhance creation, this will explain our temporary existence. Eternity may be forever, but it includes a process that can be accelerated or slowed down to a standstill by incorrect choices. In reality, time is the gravity of creation. There are days in our lives that seem to slow down to a standstill. This is usually when we are confused or uncertain. Once we resolve our difficulties, time resumes its normal pace again. As it is in creation, so it is in our everyday existence. The laws, realities, and structures of creation are reflected in every particle of the universe. Your success begins once you choose reality over illusions and myths.

Our place in creation is now a much-debated assessment. Our intelligence as a species is now a topic of heated discussions. Are our primitive emotions rendering our species as unfit to remain in creation? There are those who believe that our primitive episodes of violent rage, which once were necessary for our survival, will now become our cause of extinction. Our ability to think has also been called into question. Are we only capable of imitating others, then deceiving ourselves into believing we are thinkers? The universe that we have formed it with myths and illusions it cannot go io forever.. We must see ourselves as we are if we are to survive. Fear, denial, ego, rage, and words are all primitive attributes of our species. That the primitive need to kill to survive continues to be a part of our current level of awareness. Now we use these primitive attributes to eliminate those who question our desire to be in control. We must eliminate all control words before our species can return to reality and therefore real time once more. We are now in a cosmic dilemma: do we choose to remain a primitive species or put aside anger, greed, and the desire for power and control or do we destroy ourselves?

The gods who once were numerous, primitive gods are now all integrated into our human-created, one God. The reality is there are no gods, only the Creator. All our primitive needs have now been integrated into the need to control. The continued existence of modern humans, no matter how or why they came into creation, will determine the future of our species. If they are a part of creation, they must accept the Creator as we do. If they will not, then they will eliminate all of us from our place in the universe or they will be removed from creation under the law of miracles.

We must choose to change ourselves. The laws of creation as designed by the Creator are our last means of survival.

Our species, in reality, has nothing to show for all of our time here on this earth. We are imitators at best. We can duplicate, but have no knowledge, ability, or awareness levels to generate enough energy to make any of our creations come alive for even a blink of time. We do have the capability of destroying ourselves. But we will do this only if we choose to remain a temporary species. The final result may not be the one we want, but it may be what we need. Increases in awareness are no guarantee of increases in knowledge. We cannot amend creation to be subordinated to our awareness level. But this is exactly what we are attempting to do. We have conflicted desires. On one hand we want to be superior beings. On the other hand, we want to be primitive beings, waging war upon each other to satisfy our primitive rage. In the end all we can control is our own selves. If our Creator needs no control, and evidence proves this to be true, then surely we can acknowledge that beyond our own selves, there need be no controls.

There are those who emphatically believe that we are being controlled or observed by aliens or outside forces; we must concede that we cannot rule this out. Even if this is true, this in no way diminishes our Creator and therefore the laws of creation. No matter the source, everything is subject to the laws of the universe. The existence of all beings or matter in creation is subordinated to the designs of our Creator. Therefore, to give other beings power over you is a mistake. Only fear can make you do this.

At any rate, our Creator does not require worship: only to love and loved. As a species we fail ourselves and others when we require worship and control. We must fear control and nothing more. Therefore, to worship is to allow yourself to be controlled. It is also counter to the nature of our Creator. To believe that we can control creation is ignorance personified. To accept that we cannot is the beginning of our perfection and the difference between failure and success.

Evolution or creation? There is too much time needed for evolution and too much time needed for creation. There is evidence supporting both evolution and creation. Therefore, our concept of time may be flawed.

Time may only be in our minds. Life is forever. Where you are now may well be your forever. Choice is everything. Begin your forever now. If you feel the power within you now, just think how it will be when you experience your next level in your perfection. Life is a promise, but a promise you must choose to accept. We are given a chance to become more than humans; we must make the choice to live forever.

CHAPTER 4:
THE DISCOVERY OF YOU

You were not created by accident. You were born owing nothing to anyone other than yourself. This is your reality. In fact, there is no other reality. If you are to discover the real you, begin with the creation of you first.

You were born to love. This is a reality. Never try to change this reality. Love is yours to give.

You were not created out of nothing. There is no something for nothing. Never expect to become the real you without effort. The universe is formed based on the concept of duality. This is the perfection of it all.

The only control you have is self-control. This is all the control you will ever need. So, stop trying to control what you cannot control. This is your reality.

There are limits to reality. So, your reality is limited. Accept your limitations. This is your reality. Happiness begins once you accept you as you were created.

You are a miracle. You live in a universe of miracles. Always be expecting to experience one in your lifetime. This is your reality. Accept it.

You have within you all your success ready and waiting to be achieved. It is there for the activating. So, pray for that which is in you. Make your life a prayer. Prayers for self-knowledge will always be answered. To communicate with yourself is a prayer. It is your talk with your Creator. Meditation and prayer are the same.

You are designed to love. Do not attempt to alter this design. This is your life and your purpose. You have unlimited love to give. This is your reality.

There is no more to ask for. This is all you can have. This is you, your reality.

How To Overcome Your Fears

Fear is a primitive survival, conditional response. Remove control from your life and all your fears will fade away. You must first remove fear from your life if you are to become a success. Fear cannot thrive in reality.

Now you know it is within universal laws that you can be the person you were meant to be if you remove the fear of reality. Read the life stories of all successful people. You will find that every one of them had to discover themselves and then use reality to become the best they could be. Fear comes from feeling helpless. Fear is an illusion. No matter where you are in your life or what your circumstances may be, you are in control. Allowing anyone or any force to control you or decide for you will return fear to your daily life. Fear is not the absence of common sense or being ignorant; it is a survival mechanism of primitive humans only. Fear changes nothing. Choice removes the illusion of fear. Fear removes freedom from your life.

Life is your gift. Choice is your defining place in life. Accept your limitations. Living in reality removes all impediments to your success.

The first revelation is the empowerment of acceptance. It is the first step in your designing of you. Accept yourself because within you lies your success. Acceptance and balance are the beginning of wisdom. The discovery of both the laws of our universe and the internal laws of our souls will in the end be our happiness and success.

The law of miracles is the totality of creation. Accept it and your success will come in the now.

CHAPTER 5:

THE LOST MEANING
OF WORDS

Modern humans are experts in control through the manipulation of words, possessing the gift of choice with an awareness above any other species now known; yet they chose control rather than love. They can see and understand both abstract and simple choices which determine creation. Yet in the ultimate attempt to control, and with the gift of their newfound intelligence, they chose to transform matter into a weapon of annihilation: the ultimate evil. Why? How could they use this newfound awareness to create so much evil?

This is one of the horrible results of the use of words by modern humans. Proclaiming war as good because it is the path to peace is in itself changing the meaning of peace. The use of words that contain no meaning or love are a failure in our use of intelligence. War is one example. War is the ultimate attempt to control. The intent of war is to control through outright extermination. War is the use of intelligence to conduct evil. War is the use of intelligence to control but with no inclusion of love or wisdom. Intelligence can support evil, but intelligence does not determine which choices we make. The realization of self is the beginning of everything in our brief forms here on Earth. The less self-aware we are, the more likely we are to make incorrect choices.

Our access to reality was restricted once we began using words and languages as a means of control. Before the advent of modern humans, words were limited in meaning. This is because words were used to communicate and not to control. The same words would not now have so many different meanings if there was not the need to control. As each word changed its meaning, the new meanings created unlimited illusions and myths. This had to be because control itself is an illusion. Under the laws of perfection, anything created from nothing will return to the form it was created from. You were not created from nothing, but you have the choice to return to nothing. You have the power; you were born with it.

So many words are now created to control. We all know there is no control; therefore, these words have no meaning. All words created to control are incorrect in their meanings and therefore no more than illusions. Words having unlimited meanings are words that, in the end, have no definitions or translations other than the intent to control.

In retrospect, the legitimate question is: are modern humans the real problem? They are either superior or misfits. There is something that is not right. The corruption of words and languages has become a means of confusion and control. Once again, we see the illusions created when incorrect choices are made. Words become illusions, creating the myths we live in. This makes our day-to-day living dreaded and strained with the feeling of impending doom. Words have become a means of distorting reality. But this is only because there are far too many of us who believe that we have no choice. But it is the exact opposite.

We now have words which once served to communicate our wants and needs and yet now these same words create more confusion and alienation within us. Where are the benefits? And if there are benefits, who are these words benefiting? Are we being gaslighted? Why would we freely choose all this confusion, pain, and mental anguish? Words and language are not the causes of confusion, mental pain, or suffering, but modern humans are the source. It is apparent that control rather than choice is the blinding desire of modern humans. This desire, if not exposed for what it is, will result in the loss of ourselves. Either we choose to find a solution, or we will be choosing to be controlled.

Any words, languages, or means of communication using control in the place of correct choices will remove us from the creative process. Extinction is not what we perceive it to be. It is more like a suspension in time. We will never cease to exist once we are created. The law of miracles ensures this to be not only possible, but it is our reality. Changing the meaning of words can change perceptions but not reality. To change the meaning of the word *hate* to mean *love* may lead you to believe you love, but the reality is that you will feel hate. This hate will destroy your essence; love will never be in your existence again as long as you feel hate, although you rename it love.

The internet has opened a new portal for control, and therefore, the creations of illusions and myths. This is why this new developing technology is becoming dominant. This is the beginning of the worship of intelligence over reality. Intelligence is now being used as a substitute for true wisdom. This is but another attempt to create yet another alternate reality. Intelligence has no control over universal laws. As with all attempts to control, intelligence used to control is evil. Intelligence does make it easier to create myths and illusions, but controllers be forewarned: intelligence will eventually destroy all illusions.

The Meaning of the Word *Devil*

I had always thought the Devil to be an entity or spirit but could never understand how or why there need be more than one Creator. This is the only reality: there is but one Creator. There are no gods and lesser gods. The Creator gave life and awareness to all living things. We have found our Devil. Control is the Devil. When our species creates a god and lesser gods, we only create illusions and myths. Our species must accept and understand this fundamental concept of creation. Understanding the power of choice is the difference between living in reality or living in illusions and myths. Choice is a gift, but the reason we will not accept this gift is a mystery.

The internet is being used by modern humans as their most recent attempts to control. Words are used not to communicate or to inform but to confuse and spread fear. These primitive fears are no longer useful in the creative processes of humanity. The meaning of words must be very limited in meaning or we will become lost in confusion, a self-created universe of illusions outside of the creative processes. The universe was formed with only one reality. All illusion-creating words block this reality.

Revealing to each of us the proof of the true simplicity of creation and the perfection of a just and loving Creator is the sum of the revelations in this book. Just as the whole is the sum of its parts, this book cannot be of any meaning to you until you translate it into your reality, then combine every discovery into one truth. You have the awareness to do this; you will have then opened your mind to the bliss that is your life, your success!

There is enough now known to accurately predict that control may be our downfall unless we open our access to reality once again. Our narcissistic desire to be in control is at the root of our distorted thinking. Your deliverance is in you, and no one other than you. There will never be another you. Freely accepting this truth and seeking to discover the reality within you will forever keep you secure in creation and your never-ending journey to greater and greater awareness levels. This life in you cannot be destroyed or manipulated if you choose not to be controlled.

As our awareness has increased, words and languages have become a means of control because modern humans, even with their recently attained higher awareness levels, have chosen it to be this way. This is because words and languages as now used are a means of mind control. Modern humans have given words so many meanings that words have become confusing and almost meaningless. This is because words with unlimited meaning can be a means used in controlling reality; to deny choices by changing a word's intended meaning to unlimited meanings. Words without meanings are no more than vibrations. They lead to the unknowns; our fears of the loss of ourselves.

Modern humans are now using words and languages to control, confuse, and support their fake realities. As a result, we now live in a world of wars, social unrest, and emotional instability. We know that this is all deceptive, yet we choose to deceive ourselves into believing all is well. We believe that we have no choice, when in fact we were created with the power of choice. We cannot remove all false illusions in an instant, but we can make the choice to see ourselves as the Creator created us. We have the power to save ourselves and this is all we need. In the next few pages, we will examine several words which are now being used to reinforce our self-created myths and illusions.

The Common Good

The common good? This phrase *common good* in the dictionary reads this way: "good for the benefit or interest of all." In fact, one of the laws of creation clearly states this reality. It is the law of equity and justice: that something that is not for the good of all cannot be for the good of anyone. This means that the common good is limited to one outcome: equity and justice. This may not be the equity and justice our species continues to seek under the illusion of control.

Changing the meaning of any one word or group of words cannot change the laws of creation and therefore reality. Modern humans are using their new level of awareness to create an alternate universe by changing the meaning of words. The common good is the first word that comes to mind. The laws of creation only allow for the common good. But modern humans have changed the meaning of the common good to subvert our true reality. They have changed the meaning of the common good to have unlimited meanings. One meaning is that if something is good for those in control, then it is good for all. This is another example of the corruption of words and languages.

Words and languages were once useful in protecting us from imminent dangers. They were the means of defining our species and conveying knowledge from one generation to another. This was before modern humans incorrectly decided they could change reality by changing the meaning of words. This has had the effect of changing the understanding of choices. The end result is that now far too many of us, and therefore large parts of our society, are living in illusions formed by incorrect choices. These are unneeded and time altering choices, creating illusions and myths. How and when will modern humans wake up to what we are doing to our own selves and how it slows down our participation in creation?

The laws of the universe: no law, regulation, form of society, or any government will survive if it is not good for every living thing, not for a few or one or many, but for all. This truth we must accept and understand if we want to live in reality. The truth is that every time we attempt to create or regulate we will fail because the laws of creation allow for no control. The universe is constantly unfolding. It is now far too late to change because the laws of creation were defined perfectly by our Creator.

Perfection is perfect love; therefore, when we live within the laws of creation we will always be on our journey to a perfect awareness of love. No choice can be the correct choice unless it is the choice of all, not a selected majority. All attempts to change this law will remove us from the focus in our lives. This together with another fundamental law, that something cannot be created out of nothing, binds us together in the circle of creation for you and everyone. This reality is not subject to words. These laws cannot be changed or amended to change reality. This one law is straightforward and simple: it must be good for all or it becomes an illusion.

This means that all the laws we make, the governments we form, and the norms we select must be good for all of us or they will result in anger, anguish, and total confusion, granting control to only a few. It is important to understand that the only control our universe allows is the control we have over our own selves. No matter your future, just remember something cannot be made from nothing. Your success depends on this.

Changing the Meaning of *Kingdom*

One of the most ancient words is the word *kingdom*. The original meaning was more like a garden or a location with someone in charge, later known as the ruler. It was during this time that a new creation or a new form of humans suddenly, and seemingly spontaneously, appeared. These modern humans had a greater awareness level than any other species or living thing up to that time. They were skilled in geometry and experts in astronomy. It is not known if modern humans were the first to understand this new awareness, but they deliberately used it to make themselves gods.

Through the use of intelligence and manipulation, they converted this new knowledge handed down to them in ways that it was never intended to be used. It was during this era that the very first incorrect choices were made. This period was from five thousand to twenty thousand years ago.

Primitive humans experienced fear as a survival reflex, together with short term denial, so that fear did not freeze their ability to react in seconds. They knew that they had but two basic choices. They could fight or take flight. So, all the words they used were reality-based because they had but one meaning. Modern humans over time invented words which triggered the same fears, but these fears could be overcome by neither fight nor flight. Unfamiliar words with confusing meanings were used as control-based triggers of fear which our primitive ancestors once were able to fight or run from. But now they could not be overcome by running from them or fighting them.

As more words were invented, so were different meanings for the same word. This allowed for greater control. The word *king* was added with a new meaning. The king became the ruler, the one in control of the kingdom. Then the priests emerged. They were the creators of the illusion that the king was divine. The priests created the myths that the Creator had chosen the king. Because the king was the chosen one by the Creator, the king was perceived to be infallible and therefore no one questioned why the king had all the wealth. But there was no concern, because the king would protect the masses; therefore, none questioned these unfamiliar meanings of words.

These words would create several levels of power and wealth. Another unfamiliar word, *class*, was added and this opened the control gates. Next came the word *power*. The very next word was *laws*. In an instant we became subject to the king and then subject to the common good of the kingdom. In essence we became servants of the common good. This was the beginning of modern humans creating a god in their image, leading to the illusion that because this god did not stop the things they did, God approved their actions or was powerless to stop them. In this way the definition of common good was actually defined as what is good for the king.

Modern humans multiplied their efforts, focusing their newfound knowledge and awareness not to advance their understanding of creation but instead to control other humans. They justify this as being good for all of us. The outcome is that it is exploitation and domination of us by any realistic conclusion. Explaining or making assumptions on the reasons why modern humans decided to do this is an exercise in irrationality, because it is unreal. This is where we find ourselves now.

Modern humans have continued to seek new methods of control. The newest attempt is through technology as a means of control. The false belief that we will be able to use artificial intelligence and thereby eliminate our Creator is arrogance personified. Could it be that modern humans are mutations unable to understand creation? Their manipulation of words is evil because control is evil. Words created to control, no matter how defined, are evil.

The Many Meanings of the Word *Government*

Everyone believes that the government is our protector. If we obey and pay all our fees and taxes, we will prosper and be comforted. Without a government to take care of us, we fear that our world will crumble; then who will protect and monitor us? Our reality as we perceive it is that without control, we will experience pain and sorrow all through our lives. We will be unable to survive unless governments are set up and controlled by leaders regulating our life from the time we are born until we die. Do we not have a Creator to protect our species and take care of us? Are we creators, and so all-knowing, that we can create a more efficient universe with our own laws and regulations than the universe our Creator already has made? Reality speaks louder than our corrupted words. Governments are the creation of modern humans. Governments are illusions created when we choose to believe that something can be created out of nothing or that the few can control the many. At this time there is no equity and justice.

New Words for Hiding Control

Democracy is an illusion. Nowhere in the laws of creation will democracy become a reality, maybe an illusion but never a reality. We believe that if a certain percentage make a choice, it will be good for all. The laws of creation do not allow something to become a reality unless it is good for all of creation. If we want democracy, then we must permit everyone to have a choice. If there is one hundred percent agreement on the choice, then it becomes a law; if not, another choice must be offered until one hundred percent approve the new choice.

Are there any of us who are now reading this, accepting, and understanding this reality? It is reality based. Can we, by corrupting words, change the universe and thus creation? The laws we create will always be illusions and myths. There are no majority, no ruling classes or governments, no democracies or socialisms that can be implemented unless they are good for all and not majorities of any one segment. This is an unchangeable law of creation. We are not all equal until we accept the laws of creation.

Governments have replaced kings. This is an example of changing the meaning of a word but not the reality of the word's meaning. The meaning of the word *king* was changed to mean government. Governments are now our kings. What will the word *government* be changed to mean as attempts to control continue? Illusions cannot survive unless they are constantly replaced with more illusions. Changing the meaning of words is the genesis of our newest illusions.

The case for socialism is based upon the false belief that we have too many choices. The way to change this perceived defect was to allow no control but the government. As if by magic, once we all are forced to choose only to work for the good of others then the defects of human nature would thereby be altered. This is servitude under the name of socialism, the ultimate attempt to control. The reality is that the laws of creation already provide for our needs to live together in cooperation and progress in the creative processes. It again seems so easy to understand and accept, but we will not. It may be that our species is not as wise and all-knowing as we think we are. This may be the reason why we choose myths and illusions rather than reality. If this is true, then we have created our own laws; universal laws are put aside. We are indeed the creators. If we believe this, then all is lost.

All forms of government, democracy, socialism, rulers, and monarchies have replaced religions. All are examples of changing the meanings of words to sustain and continue to create illusions. We will surely fail if we choose to worship any entities, because to worship is to accept control. We are born free; life is free. Why? Because life is and forever even if we deny it.

Words with Ever Changing Meanings

There are those in control who believe that we possess the ability to control and change the morals and ethics which are inherent in human nature. The truth is the only power we have is to make our own choices. These choices will place burdens on us until we make correct choices. The sooner we make the discovery of the power of correct choices, the sooner we will be free again. The universe we live in is ours with no strings or conditions attached. All we are required to do is choose to accept it as it is. Even if all of our species thinks we must pay a price, the truth is that in reality there is no price to pay; it is ours, free for the choosing.

The cost of trying to change a perfect creation and its laws will be an existence outside of creation with the results being isolation, loneliness, and frustrations. This is the cost of denial. Everything is a choice. Our species cannot create or regulate. We can only choose. This is our power. The Creator is love; because of this love, we each were given the gift of choice. So be ready for a new life when you choose to accept this gift. Words do not make reality. Actions can restore reality. Saying one thing and doing another is living a lie. A lie is nothing more than an attempt to control.

Words can be beautiful. They allow us to express our emotions. Words give us songs that warm the heart. Words band us together as one. Words lift us up with love and kindness. The use of words can supply all the feeling and entertainment we desire without the risk of bodily injuries to our physical beings, where our life flows through. Reality-based words can transform humans to become more like our Creator. This is the miracle given to every one of us. There is no doubt if we choose to use words and languages in this way, the Creator will raise us up to a higher level of awareness. All we need to do is choose to do it! Then leave fear behind. Discard old emotions, myths, and illusions. Just do it! Control is the Devil. Control is the survival plan of modern humans. But it is a flawed plan because it is based upon total control. We must expose modern humans for what they are. Instead of worshipping them, we must eliminate them.

This is a good place to take a moment to think about what is known and that which is yet to be known. There is enough now known to be true that we can employ this new knowledge to make correct choices. One known truth is that all humanity is at a special place in creation. If we allow ourselves to be used for the benefits and survival of other humans, then there is no future for primitive humans in the creative process. If indeed our species is a hybrid of ancient humans and modern humans, and if this cannot be resolved, then we are now on the path to becoming only a temporary species.

Each species has a purpose in creation. As of now the purpose we have chosen is to kill, oppress, and enslave our own species. There is no place in creation for living lifeforms which exist for the sole purpose to kill, live off of, or enslave their own kind. If this is true, then our reason for existence is to remove our species from creation. This is reason enough for us to choose to change and do it now! This alone should make it crystal clear to our species that we are very close to becoming useless in the process of the perfection of our creation. From the existence of recorded time until now there have been more than one hundred and thirty wars. Why? This is a horrible reason purpose for our species. We must acquire wisdom or all is lost. No entity can survive if its purpose is to destroy itself. In this universe life cannot be destroyed. But entities based on destruction of others or themselves will have life no more, because they destroy the balance needed to remain useful.

Our continuing attempts to create an illusionary Creator of vengeance and anger is a futile attempt to justify our desire for control. The correct choices can be found in the laws of creation. To believe that changes are not needed is to surrender to a lower level of awareness and settle for a lifetime of pain, control, and oppression.

We have this power: the power of choice. The Creator is love. Those who choose not to love, when making that choice, are thereby rejecting the Creator. Love has only one meaning: it is perfection or the journey to perfection, running through our very existence. The Creator is perfect. We are life and life is love. No matter which meaning we give the word love, we cannot, by choice, alter or change it. We may define love by any other definition we choose, but it will be our definition and convey our meaning only. Devine love is defined as love with no control. We have love within us but rage destroys love. Love is a state of being and not expressed in any words or forms. Words are for use in the creative processes only but never for conveying fear, to control, or to kill other humans. Sounds and vibrations are a part of the creative process but sounds and vibrations can never be used by our species to control. Control cannot exist in creation. Control can only exist in an illusion. Because we have choices, we can exist in myths and illusions. Creation is a journey to perfection. Control is not a part of love.

A rose is the portrait of beauty. You know a rose when you smell and see one. If those in control rename a rose a weed and you make the incorrect choice to accept this false perception, the result is that you will destroy all the roses in your garden. Then no matter the illusion, the reality is that you will end up with a garden of weeds.

Control by any other name is control. Control is our Devil. The Devil by any other name is nevertheless the same personification of control. Therefore, when we accept control in any form, we accept the Devil. Now we know the origin of the Devil. So why choose control? Control is evil personified. The truth is there are no Devils, no angels, no kingdoms, they all are illusions and myths. Creation is all that is lasting. We live in creation. Creation is our all and everything. So why not choose it and accept it with its limitations? Live in it and embrace it, knowing that we cannot control reality. That which the Creator has made no species can put under their own control because love and control cannot coexist in creation. But love conquers all and will prevail. Once we truly love we will triumph. Love is in no need of control because love has no limits. When we love, we are travelers on the journey to our perfection.

Words are only as effective as we choose them to be. This is another way of saying that words are a matter of choice, making correct or incorrect choices. This being true proves that our species has made far too many incorrect choices in words. It is not what we say, it is the meaning we give our words.

Contrary to traditions and myths, words are the creation of our species. Once we gained awareness above the level of primitive humans, words have limited our choices and therefore our understanding of creation and our Creator. We have wasted our life and blocked access to love by making the choices to use words to control. It is so easy to know life. Life is our Creator living in us and through us. The Creator does not force life on any part of creation. Humans must choose life, and it is ours for a lifetime and in some form forever. It is no great mystery that we love life. Life is love. The mystery continues to be, why does our species choose control rather than love? Life is our choice. It is free. Life is a journey to perfection. Perfection is a state of love to the limit, true bliss. Our paradise is here every day, if only we will see it and not turn our eyes away. Wanting more when there is no more removes the joy of our Creator's life that runs through our being.

Love

No other word has ever been used so much to control as the word love. Think about it. The word love, when given any other meaning, is a control word. The only meaning of the word love is perfection. Perfection is the path that our Creator designed for us to follow. When the word love means perfection, it is unconditional with no strings attached; then it is love. It is not love when we love but we require something in return. Do we not see that this is what love is? Our Creator loves us in this way. If we will not accept the laws of creation, and thereby our Creator, we will never experience love.

If you do not take away anything else from this revelation, make it this: love is perfection. Believing that we love when we seek to make others in our image will not enable us to feel love. We will only feel the burden of control. When we say we love our Creator, it is meaningless if this love is not expressed with our total being, unconditional and wanting nothing in return. We are telling a universal lie when we tell ourselves that we must give up our lives to serve others. Why? Because when we serve others, we are thereby giving up ourselves to be controlled. The reality is that only when we serve others without asking for anything in return will we be truly serving others. It is a universal truth; no one who loves you will ever try to control you.

We all think we know what love is. But love is much more than feelings. The love we feel in our physical bodies is the essence of our created selves. Universal love can only be felt in the soul. This can only be experienced when we are in a state of perfection. This is just one lesson that our Creator wants us to learn. This is the truth: the more we love the less we need to control. A simple concept, yet far too many refuse to understand and live this way. We are near a turning point in our brief existence. We have the choice to learn and experience all creation, but we must first choose to believe.

The Changing Meanings of the Word Religion

Our species has used religion not to understand and be one with the Creator, but to form a god or god-humans, all designed to redo creation, subordinated to our desire to control. It appears that at this time our species cannot or chooses not to understand and accept the Creator and the laws of creation. Modern humans have given up the life of happiness and fulfillment inherent in our creation for the illusion of control. If religion is to become relevant, religion must change because it cannot be effective or relevant using methods of force, fear, punishments, or controls. In all our illusions and myths, we have named and personified control, denying it by calling it the Devil and other names. No matter the words we use, the meaning never changed; control by any other name is control. Control is devious. If we desire to live a full life and to remain in creation, we must accept that the only sin is attempting to control. Control is our Devil. Removing the choice and desire to control will change your life immediately and increase your awareness level. You will be in the real universe now and forever.

What is religion as we have fashioned it? Religion as we have defined it reflects our species as we choose to be and nothing more. Let us go into this in more detail and find out why this is. It is not religion when we use religion as an excuse to satisfy our egos and our fears of loss of control. Our species has twisted the meaning of religion. This is the fault of our species, not religion. We have complicated religion, making it multidimensional. We have made religion a maze which denies choice by making choice irrelevant. The never-ending illusionary gods that must be pleased end up being more about control and therefore more about illusions than reality.

The meaning of the word religion, as our species has chosen to employ it, requires a complete denial of reality. If we continue to place ourselves superior to the Creator and the laws of creation, we will lose everything we have created because our created purpose is not to create an alternate universe. If this is our choice, it will be an incorrect choice. The penalty for incorrect choices is already included in the laws of creation. There is no pain or suffering under the laws of creation. Just the nothingness of myths and illusions. There is no sin that we must punish or no laws, rules, or regulations which we can create that will endure, unless they are good for all of our species, and not for any one or a select few. Anything we create must not be contrary to reality or in defiance of the laws of creation. Each time we attempt to do this we create illusions and myths. Just because we can create something out of nothing does not make it any more than nothing. It can only create an illusion. We are only slowing down the processes of creation, but we will never change it. The laws of creation are so comprehensive that we can make incorrect choices because the law of miracles includes incorrect choices. We are all part of the circle of creation. The law of miracles makes this circle unbreakable forever by Creator design.

There are two words: faith and belief. The definition of *faith* is to base your life on the unknown. The definition of *belief* is to accept the laws of the universe and a perfect Creator. The use of words to control is apparent when the meanings of faith and belief reflect the use of control. Faith is based on what might be. Belief is based only on what is. What might be needs to be constantly controlled. What is, needs no control.

The Meanings of Words in Creation

Once our species makes the correct choice to remain in creation by accepting the Creator and then choosing to remain in creation, there will be no death as we know it. The real death is to live our existence outside of creation. This death can only occur and be final if we make the choice to control. We are meant to be eternal, but it is our choice. All are called but we must make a choice to accept. Our Creator is perfect. Love is a state of perfection. Our Creator is love; therefore, if our choice is to love, then we cannot go wrong. The correct choice for our species is to accept that our Creator created us to love. You can do this, I can do this, and anyone or all of us can do this. Do this and experience a lifetime of fulfillment and sense of being.

This change in our culture has been in the process for the last five thousand years. It has been a gradual but persistent attempt to return our species to primitive beings serving those in control. But we were the chosen ones. We were the ones given geometry. Locate the culture given the knowledge of geometry and you will discover who we really are.

The final stages of complete control are now getting ever closer. Are we too blind to see? Our species believes in fate when in many instances it is really our choice.

The Word Government Is Our New Religion

Our Creator has been replaced with a new god; a god offering a new universe composed of human-made laws, the majority of which contradict, or void out each other. This new god is now called government. At the center of this religion is the belief that life does not matter. The gift of individual creation is defined as a weakness in humanity. The government is the personification of our new reality and creator of a new world, a world that does not include our Creator. Prayers are now called taxes. Donations are required to gain access to these newly self-created gods. Even with all these methods of control, we can remain in control by refusing to choose to be controlled. This is the power we have to change ourselves and claim our Creator once again. Then forever we will be all that we were created to become.

Remember this: words are not needed as we now use them in creation. The Creator was and is perfection. Therefore, words are primitive responses used only in the illusion of denial. Words that are not limited in meaning are control words. We must bring back words that are formed to comply with the laws of creation. We can do this now but only if we choose them.

Governments are now in control. Government is our new religion. This is the true reality. Control is evil. Our government controls us. If our government would only give us back our individual self-control, all governments would be good. The religion that governments have become is the most recent attempt at total control.

The government has changed the word money to exercise control over all of us. Those who produce must work for those who pay them with illusions. Remove illusion from government and government will have a purpose. Without purpose nothing can last.

There is one truth that we all can understand and accept. Changing the meaning of money as a measure of exchange has created a means of control which, if not corrected, will be the end of our species. Money must return to a verifiable valuation.

It should be noted that we have no valid understanding of why we speak so many different words and languages. We also have no valid understanding why words have different meanings in various locations on our planet Earth. Take time and think this over. This is counter to creation and the wisdom of our Creator. Could it be that words and languages have only one purpose; to control?

Challenge; become a thinker.

CHAPTER 6:
HUMAN NATURE

The result of our species choosing to create a universe without choices will be the end of us unless we change this incorrect choice. The first correct choice we must make is to change our belief that we are the creators with our gods as our servants. We were created to serve ourselves and seek love above all. This is a concept we must make ourselves understand before we can attain any self-satisfaction or peace in our lives. Even self-love can be harmful to our being if it never goes beyond self-worship. Worship is never needed to attain your life goals; only first love, then acceptance. But will we choose to do this? Are we self-aware enough? The false reality most of us have chosen to live in is no longer workable in the future of us all.

A quick assessment will provide you with more insight and proof of this human failing, if indeed it turns out to be our failure. We must remember that nothing is certain because of our gift of choice. Everything in creation has a purpose. But balance determines the future existence of everything in creation. A successful life is a balanced life.

We justify all our faults with a distorted, narcissistic narrative. In a contorted way, we are proud of our faults. We blame our failures on our human nature. Why are we this way? Denial is not a solution. Every time we choose denial, we create an illusion. Do we have personality defects? Something is not right with us or too many of us. Is it our human nature at fault or is our true human nature being suppressed?

Blaming or justifying our shortcomings to be the fault of our human nature is an example of the primitive thinking which our species must reject and replace with the reality that we have no excuses, because we were created to rise above our human natures. There is no shame to be found in creation. Knowing all this, the question is: will we access our new place in creation? Will we become more than primitive beings, or will we never be more than animals? There are no indications at this moment in time that we can or will choose to become more than primitive humans. We cannot aspire to become perfect if we are not willing to leave our primitive nature behind and transition to a higher level as we were created to do. This is true for each of us; we are not defective. We cannot become all that we were created to be if we are not willing to leave our primitive fears behind. In our quest for success, we must understand that success is not defined entirely by the accumulation of things but almost entirely on the enjoyment of life and the discovery of our success. We can survive as long as we have a purpose, so we must choose our purpose with wisdom.

The voices we hear or, more exactly, the thoughts flashing and pulsating in our consciousness, where do they originate from? Are they helpful or do they come from the incorrect choices made for us over thousands of years? Are we thinking or being programmed to allow others to do our thinking? We all know this concept to be true: we become what we think. Yet we do not question these thoughts and where or how they originated.

Our thoughts will never determine our existence or change reality, only our choices. This is reality; negative thoughts limit or take away our freedom to choose correctly. When we reject creation, primitive thoughts and fears dominate our being, making us less than humans. Human nature is not the reason for our failures; it is the controlling nature of modern humans. We are animals no longer, that is, if we choose not to be. The choice is ours. Modern humans' desire to indiscriminately destroy other humans and change reality makes them of no purpose, thus removing them from creation.

This is a good place to ask this valid question: are humans narcissistic, and if so, then why? What are the attributes of narcissistic disorder? Let us examine each one, then ask if this might be the personality disorder of modern humans. There are several signs and symptoms in determining a narcissistic personality disorder. Here are several listed below.

Unreasonable Expectations

We need a God who exists to serve our needs and magical expectations, like a genie in a bottle. We always want more and are constantly disappointed and not ever content. We live on a planet filled with beautiful oceans and mountains and beneath a golden moon, backed up by uncountable sparkling bright stars on our nightly horizon, yet we want something even more spectacular and more centered on our idealization of self. Creation itself is not enough. Creation, to be valid, must be all about us and our ever-increasing expectations. We must be the center at all times. We even reject this earthly Garden of Eden, proclaiming we possess knowledge greater than our Creator. This was the illusion which created the myth that we were driven out from this garden in some mystical heaven, thereby denying that we are in reality in a beautiful garden in the now. How will we ever be content as long as we want more than can be? Not in this lifetime or ever for that matter.

A World of Illusions and Magical Thinking

If reality does not please us, we deny it. We accept wars as necessary. This is how the good among us ensure peace and survival: by fighting wars. We kill, calling killing the survival of the fittest, but in reality, we kill out of our need to control. This distortion of reality, that good can do evil to destroy evil, is a classic myth and nothing more than an illusion. Those of us who cannot understand this reality are living in a magical universe reinforced with myths, one that humans cannot remain in, notwithstanding our illusions. We create a magical universe with our thoughts and then attempt to transform them into a material universe through the use of control.

There Are Always Strings Attached

This is counter to the laws of creation. The Creator gave all living things choices; choices with no strings attached. We believe that our Creator gives out love but attaches the condition that we be both obedient and constantly be in fear that this love may be taken away from us. The Creator has no needs, therefore the Creator's gift to our species is the gift of choice. There are no conditions or strings attached.

Narcissistic Injury

If we find ourselves feeling intense anger or even rage when our false beliefs are not validated or when boundaries are put in place by reality, we may be narcissistic. Anger and rage are a danger to our species. We must remove anger and rage, or creation cannot live within our souls. Rage is common among primitive humans.

Total Disregard of Others

A willingness to allow those around you to die or suffer, provided you are happy and in control, is a narcissistic trait common to all who possess a narcissistic disorder.

Questions That Must Be Answered

The above are attributes of a narcissistic personality. Is it within reason to think modern humans exhibit this disorder. This is profound and revealing, filled with warnings for our species' place in reality and therefore creation.

We must consider the possibility that modern humans possess narcissistic personalities. If we do, the question becomes why? Personalities functioning with this disorder suffer arrested development coming from neglect, lack of love, berating, and other abuses during their early years. What about our earlier years? This disorder is a coping mechanism, which is in essence the destruction of self as a way of existing and is a disconnected means of self-survival. Could it be that modern humans or other forces are not allowing our species to be ourselves and thereby forcing us to serve them? Are they living using our energy and life forces? We know something is not feeling right. We must choose to take back who we are and our place in creation. The reality is that we can, but the fear of the loss of control renders too many of us without any identity in creation.

As difficult as it may be, our species must see our faults. The next step in our level of awareness is to choose to modify our human nature in order to move up to our next level of existence. There must be urgency because we are nearing the point of no return; reality will not wait forever. Primitive humans are becoming increasingly pushed aside by the illusions created by modern humans or other forces and entities.

We must accept the laws of the Creator. Our correct choices are unlimited. But every choice we make has consequences. Our species does not have unlimited incorrect choices. This is true for all living things. In creation there are only correct choices if we are to remain in creation. Our species has the gift of choice, granted by the Creator. Each correct choice we make moves us closer to the Creator as we move closer to our unique self. Incorrect choices move us deeper into myths and illusions. Correct choices must be the answer, because incorrect choices violate all laws of creation by eliminating balance. There can be no purpose without balance, and without purpose all things fade away.

Human Nature and Control

How are we ever going to understand creation, and the Creator or the path to our perfection in this life, if every choice we make must be based according to our need to be in control? By terrorizing and demanding that no one challenge the incorrect choices we make, we will only force ourselves into nothingness and never-ending fears.

Even if you reject the thought that our species is not the center of creation, and even if you feel we are creators, I am sure you will discover that we must make correct choices, hopefully not too late. Without correct choices, nothing will improve no matter what we choose. Being the most powerful does not matter. Why? Because creation is not based on power or control. The Creator is love. The Creator is life, and we are life. Therefore, to be alive we must conform with creation. There are no other choices.

Human nature is not an excuse or reason to make us ashamed of who we are. We are not condemned at birth as our self-created myths and illusions force us to believe. Humans are a kind-natured, loving, and caring species. We must choose to reject every control placed upon us by choosing who we really are, and thereby reclaim our lives and dignity and thereby our places in creation. Modern humans must find a way to become one of us or they cannot survive. If they do not or will not, we have the power of correct choices to eliminate them. We can choose our life because creation is on our side. There are no other choices. Either modern humans must choose the path that creation intended for our species or they will not last. Our place in creation is ours to choose. This truth is not complicated or difficult to determine. The truth is that the laws of the Creator are the only laws. Our species cannot serve both our Creator and those in control. We must choose the Creator, not those of us wanting to be in control.

The first step is removing fear from our minds. Fear is the basis of control. Choose the Creator and the laws of creation then all will be well. Consider all the fears our species live under each day. We can remove these fears from our lives just by choosing to reject all forms of life that seek to control us. Control does not exist in the laws of creation, just cause and effect. Either reality or oblivion. Love does not inflict pain. If our species is so out of touch with creation that we risk oblivion, then we will have failed to understand our new level of awareness. Pain and suffering are the results of control, not a loving Creator. The answer is right before our eyes. We must replace human nature with a new level of awareness. We can do this by letting go of our fear of losing control. Control is an illusion.

The myth that we are born unworthy to be in this world is based on the illusion of control. The myth of original sin is based on the illusion of control. The illusion of control continues to depend on the creation of never-ending myths. This grandiose quest by our species for control continues to be the source of these illusions and myths. The fear of losing control is a part of human nature that we must choose to reject. Our species has new powers, but we must choose them. Illusions will always be ours to choose. The truth and the way are right before our eyes; there is no control in creation.

Are we so self-centered that we are doing this to ourselves or are a small percentage of our species the perpetrators? Our species now chooses to believe there are unlimited gods, all under the control of one God. This reduces the Creator to a powerless entity subject to innumerable deficiencies which only our species can remove. If this is true, then the Creator becomes nothing more than an observer unable to come to our assistance. Thus, creation is reduced to the choices of the many based on the choices of those in control. The result is that a segment of our species become controllers of all our species. The laws of creation will not allow any choices which are not for the benefit of all of creation. Therefore, only an illusion is created. Until our species accepts the laws of creation, we will continue to be living in a life of illusions and myths.

Continuing to believe that we have the power to create is self-centered and narcissistic. Anger or denial will not change the reality of the unchanging laws of creation. Now is a good place to state a binding law of creation: all choices made will be incorrect choices if they are not good for everyone. Every human being must understand and accept this law of creation, or our species will not remain in creation. The notion that without our control the laws of creation will fail is an illusion in itself. We must let go. Control is contrary to all the laws of creation. Just to make it simple and easy for our species to understand, control is evil. We call control the Devil.

This is an example of it all: our species has created a list of sins, laws, and regulations. For each one we violate or fail to adhere to, we have created penalties. We believe that if we do not do so, the Creator cannot continue to exist .How can we profess our belief in the Creator on one hand and on the other believe that we must control the Creator's own creation? Will we ever, as a species, increase our awareness to comprehend the reality that control is an illusion? This book will give you all you need to know about reality and prove to you that no control is ever needed for you to live the life our species was created to experience. These are the facts. We must accept the truth. Until we try living according to the laws of creation, we will never experience how good life can be. Living in illusions may appear to be real, but the feeling of reality is more satisfying than any illusions. Do you seriously believe that modern humans can determine who you are and who you were created to become? Your happiness and success depend on your formation of self; nothing more will work for you.

Our True Nature

I have come across speculations giving explanations on the origins of modern humans. I do not believe it matters what we choose to believe, creatures from outer space, mutations, or other forces unknown. No matter our origin, everything in creation is subject to the same universal laws designed by our Creator. We are in a safe place when we accept the universe around us and the universe within us.

Narcissistic Abuse

We must face up to this distinct phenomenon: are we victims of narcissistic abuse? Those who suffer narcissistic abuse were never treated with love and kindness in early childhood. As a result, they had to deny reality to survive. If they cannot be in control, they go into a meltdown. They use gaslighting to avoid reality. They have no persona, so they create a personality out of nothing to maintain their ability to live in denial. They use intimidation to control those around them. They are never at fault; in fact, they are always the victim. And finally, they are self-absorbed. It is all about them, who they are, and what they want. Are we abuse victims? This is the enigma surrounding modern humans.

We cannot rely on religion, superstition, scientific conclusions, or any other dogmas to save us from our participation in false realities. In the final analysis, it is all about you and I and where we find ourselves in the now. First, each of us must find our true reality and discover who we are, and only then will we be able to begin the process of designing our life. The survival of our species depends on each of us. We are primitive beings no more. This is our reality. We cannot go back. We can only become extinct. Worshiping any other of our species or our self-created gods is allowing ourselves to be controlled.

We are no longer animals. Our survival no longer depends on conquering our surroundings. We must now conquer ourselves. We must discover our new purpose. This will be our individual success as well as the survival of our species.

Our transformation from animals to superior entities is not predetermined. This will require much more love and acceptance of our realities. All will be lost if we do not make this choice.

CHAPTER 7:

SCIENCE

Science is a word with many meanings. But in practice science has been used by modern humans for other influences. Science is the study of the structure of the physical and natural world through the use of perception and assumptions. Science can be beneficial. But if we choose science as a religion, thereby treating science as a means of control, we will find ourselves living in an illusion once again. Control is not part of the creative process. Choice is, but control is not. Science has become more of a means of control at ever-increasing levels during the past two thousand years.

In the name of science, modern humans pushed reason aside and inserted a new set of laws and illusions. As always, our species readily accepted these controls because of our insatiable need for control. Control always blocks out reality. Why was so much anger and hate suddenly generated between us? Science cannot create. Our species are not creators. Everything in our human experience becomes lost when we attempt to control. Reality cannot be changed by thoughts, denials, or suppressed by anger and rage. Science can only be useful in creation if we redirect it to understanding the universe as it is, not as we choose it to become.

As a culmination of thousands of years, the number of illusions began to increase, and now more illusions continue to increase at a malignant pace. This changed the use of science from understanding creation into the use of science to control us.

True science is a study of the universe and the structure of the laws of creation. This is from the beginning to where creation is in the now. Removing the elements of control will once again return science to be a benefit for our species. It will always be true that nothing can be revealed stating the unknown as the known. Our purpose was not to use science to recreate the universe. Our purpose is to create our universe within ourselves. Our importance cannot be anything other than this. We are created for a purpose. For now, we are the chosen ones. We are a transitional species. We are the first to be given this choice. Our place in creation will be our choice.

Science must include the spiritual dimensions of creation, or it will be no more than an observation and outline of matter.

CHAPTER 8:

MATHEMATICS

We have used mathematics to measure the universe and the passing of time; the projection of numbers and decimals from now to infinity. But has our mathematics created anything? Mathematics has created the abstract measurement of the universe, time, numbers, and space, none of which have been successful in our understanding of creation other than supporting speculations. In every instance where mathematics has attempted to control, the results have been devastating. The atomic bomb is the most horrendous result thus far. Mathematics have produced enough formulas and equations to fill enough chalkboards and mathematical papers and transcripts to fill our continually expanding illusionary universe. Yet mathematics will never create anything other than copies and abstracts of our illusionary desires. The danger for our species is that we might choose the illusion of control that mathematics offers.

The truth is that mathematicians are concluding increasingly that numbers and equations validate the existence of the Creator and the laws of creation. This is because our species is slowly discovering that there is no control to be found in numbers and equations. Recent attempts at placing quotas and limits using numbers and equations to regulate human behavior have all failed. Once our species rejects all efforts to control, mathematics will enhance our creation as our Creator provided for within the laws of creation.

It is unbelievable that our species is unable to comprehend that we cannot change or control creation by imposing numbers and equations on our perception of creation and the creative processes. The laws of creation are not determined by learned professors or mathematics but only though our understanding and living within these laws.

Mathematics can increase our understanding of creation and reshape some forms of matter, but once mathematics attempts to predict or change the future or to create new forms of matter and thereby attempts to enable controls, it drifts into false realities.

Mathematics has a purpose, but once control becomes the purpose, mathematics becomes of no use. We must never think that mere numbers and formulas determine creation.

CHAPTER 9:
GEOMETRY

The realization of our new awareness originated with the gift of geometry. Geometry is a validation of the design of creation and the laws of the universe. This is because it does not contain illusions, myths, and speculations. It is a study of what is and not what might have been. It requires no mythical stories to support the realities embedded in its theorems and formulars and postulates.

As a young student, I sensed the realities that geometry validated and yet how simple and powerful were these insights. I came to realize this to be true because geometry is the profile of creation and is based upon the self-limiting laws of creation. One of the great mysteries is why our species has never used the concepts of geometry to improve our place in creation but instead used mathematics and science in our attempts to alter the universe.

Geometric theories and formulas never change or need adjusting. This is because the Creator is perfect and thus the Creator's designs are never in need of changing. This is the essence of geometry. This cannot be said of science and mathematics. Science and mathematics are constantly being manipulated and changed. Both are currently being used to change thoughts and perceptions. This is because, by constantly changing the variables in science and mathematics, modern humans use them to control our own species and construct false assumptions as an alternative to reality. Changing reality is not possible as it is outlined in the laws of creation. That which our Creator has already created cannot be amended or changed. Our attempts to alter creation will only create myths and illusions.

Geometry was our first awareness of knowledge and wisdom. This new awareness began during the advent of ancient humans. This was before the desire to control entered our awareness. Somehow, we have lost our access to our intended selves and replaced it with our desire to control; something has been lost in translation. We must find this awareness once again and include this knowledge and understanding in our lives and never try to change it or adjust it ever again. When we choose to do this, we will indeed become all the Creator intended. Life without choice is less than living. It is the difference between living and breathing and living in a bubble looking through a one-sided mirror, seeing without the benefit of feeling—except the anger and the pain of the removal of our free spirits. Why did we suddenly choose the illusion of control? Did we suddenly transform to a level of awareness which we were not able to comprehend or understand? There has to be a reason. The survival of humans may depend on us finding the reason or reasons.

The theorems of straight lines, circles, and postulates all represent and fall within the laws of creation. Mathematics and sciences have become attempts to control, simulate, or change our social perceptions. Therefore, they only create illusions. All illusions require myths to survive.

Our Creator, with the gift of geometry, revealed to us everything there is now known, which will increase our awareness level and advancement and assure that we remain in our limited place in the creative process. But our species, or a distinct number of us, decided to go it on our own. In short, we thought and continue to think that we are the creators of our Creator. As a result, our place in creation is in question, and we are in danger of becoming no more than illusions and myths, removed from creation and suspended in time until creation cleanses itself of our false realities.

Geometry is the blueprint of creation. It does not matter which size or shape; a straight line is the shortest distance between the beginning and the destination. This is one of the laws of creation the Creator chose. It is a part of reality and never needs change or adjustments. The law that the entirety is the sum of its composition is another law of creation. This is the law that clearly states that no control can be part of the entirety of creation. Once our species becomes aware of this law of creation, we will have the power we have been seeking but never found. This will be our gift.

Geometry was the first gift we were granted when we entered our new level of awareness. It was intended to be our steppingstone to our next level of awareness. Geometry is our key in obtaining understanding and knowledge. Before our species can go to a higher level of awareness, we must master the concept of creation as it is embedded in the full understanding of the concepts and foundations of geometry. But as usual, our species has chosen or allowed others to choose for us, thus rejecting the creation concepts in geometry to replace them with our own mathematics, equations, and theories. It is the same process for science. The results are terrifying. What ignorance or arrogance is this? This is discouraging because geometry was included with our new awareness, but we pushed it aside. Apparently because we thought ourselves suddenly able to change reality when we clearly are not.

CHAPTER 10:
YOUR CHOICES BECOME YOU

A slave believes there is no choice but to remain a slave. The reality is that servitude is a choice. Yes, even slavery is a choice. Slavery of any kind is temporary if the choice is made not to accept being a slave. Facing reality and the truth is the beginning of self-discovery. The effect of outer circumstances and conditions cannot change the reality that you were created with the power of choice. It is not about heredity or environment. It is all about correct choices and incorrect choices.

We are born unique, with our own limited potential. Our first choice is to accept this truth or reject this power. Once we choose to believe that we are slaves to any control of other humans, we must invent myths and illusions to make ourselves feel justified for making this choice. Each and every time we try to control or allow ourselves to be controlled we are no longer our real selves. When we accept slavery in any form we are in an alternate universe and therefore no longer a part of reality. Should we remain in this state for any reason, we will no longer be the entity we were created to become.

But under the law of miracles, the life we rejected will be part of the unfolding of creation, but no longer ours as it could have been. This is the result of our choosing to live in illusions. All illusions fall apart when the myths that support them are exposed. These myths were made out of nothing; therefore, they will return to nothing. The gift we have been given is that we can choose reality at any time. Reality never changes, and it can never be enhanced or be in need of myths and illusions to be enjoyed. Once we experience reality, our satisfaction will continue to refresh itself again and again. When we choose to try to recreate reality or ourselves, we enter into unsustainable illusions. Control never works. Creation does not function through the use of control. This concept must be accepted and understood by modern humans. If we do not, our species will only be a temporary part of creation. A part we may one day understand but it will be too late for so many. We will never attain success if we make the choice to be enslaved.

There is no free will, only free choice, or for that matter, there is no fate, only our limited successes. All creation is subject to limitations. Free will and fate are both subject to the laws of miracles and all the other universal laws of creation. The power of choice is the source of who we are intended to become. Understanding the power of choice in the end determines our individual fates. Our freedom to choose can in no way change our limitations.

Our individual creations give us control, but of our own self only. We cannot control others, just our own created self. The Creator created a perfect creation based upon love. We can know this love and experience our place in creation if we make the choice to love; so few choose to love. Our species stubbornly believes that we can both control and define good, but this is not true. Even if we refuse to consider this truth, our place in creation is dependent upon choosing this reality. It is as if we are saying creation is defective and we must remake it or change it. Rage and anger results when we lose self-control. Ever wonder why there is so much anger and rage all around us? To control or be controlled is the source of all anger, rage, frustrations, and unhappiness, all of which must be eliminated if we are ever going to experience our success.

There is no disputing the significance of our perceptions. But reality is most certainly very different than our illusions. Until our species accepts the laws of creation, our perceptions will continue to enable us to live in a false reality of our own making, signifying nothing. Denying reality is the cause of our anger and rage, all the maladjustments and emptiness in our lives.

Our Creator formed creation in a manner that limits everything to within the circle of infinity. Our clear challenge is to simply choose to accept and remain in creation. This is all we need to know. Our essence is, from the beginning, an ever-expanding entity forming an ever-expanding life circle, until we fade away or we enter our next level in the ever-expanding circle of creation.

The notion that the universe will cease to be if our species were not in control is inexplicable and based upon our exaggerated egos. The only basis for these magical beliefs appears to be our attempts to overcome the fear of having no control. The perception of control is a primitive reflex. Seeking an existence based on control is only a temporary state and not a means of forming your life. Our species must move beyond primitive survival instincts and accept the truth that no control is needed. If we remove control and replace it with correct choices, everything in our individual existence will unfold—all within the limitations of creation.

Success is not unlimited. The universe is not unlimited. Success may be defined simply as choosing your soul to live within the circle of creation until your perfection is attained. Happiness may be defined as accepting yourself and living within the constraints of the laws of the universe. Choosing the laws of the universe will result in you living forever. Your form does not matter; your life does.

You Can Choose Success

Success is attainable in your lifetime. We are spiritual beings temporarily in a human body, composed of energy and matter. We spend too much time wondering why, when the best time spent would be wondering how.

The reason why there is so much frustration is that we are never shown the way before us. Our myths and illusions hide reality and leave us empty inside. Our purpose is hidden in the alternate dimensions of control. Balance is not maintained. There is no concept of balance. Our universe is held together by balance. Because of the duality of the universe, if balance is not maintained there is no purpose. This is for each of us and for the entire universe as we know it. This is the very reason why control cannot function in reality. Nothing comes without effort. Begin by choosing the laws of creation.

Once our souls are newly created through the law of miracles, we are allowed to assume a new body with a chance to experience and learn more about ourselves and love; we are allowed to choose the purpose of our existence. This is our guarantee that once we make the correct choices our success will be certain. Just remember that there can be no success until we both understand and accept all the laws of creation. Success is temporary; life is forever. Success gives pleasure along the way. Life gives perfect love, leaving no more desires that cannot be experienced.

CHAPTER 11:
DEATH IS A MYTH

Our species, as far as we know, is the most aware. The most advanced on this planet Earth. But with all the awareness we have, our self-awareness is our weakness, the total absence of it. We are far more prideful and arrogant than self-aware. We worship our own versions of creation and we have made up our own religions. We worship control. Control is our Devil. Our actions indicate that far too many of us do not believe there is a Creator. Then too many of us choose to believe that we are gods. We are free to choose this perception within the constraints included in the universal law of miracles. But choice has everything to do with it.

There is no death as we perceive it to be under the universal law of miracles, only transformation. Does a flower die? We witness it grow to its perfection and then fade away once again. But under the law of miracles, it comes back again for us to behold in all its beauty. Death, as we have formed it to be, is a myth created by our own species. The life assigned to each of us is eternal, but it is our choice to embrace it in all its wonder or return it to our Creator. The universal law of miracles ensures that life will never be removed from creation. Death is a myth. We readily accept that matter, once created, cannot be destroyed. The law of miracles makes it possible for our life, once created, to last forever. Our Creator gave us the law of miracles. We will be forever, but only our Creator will determine the how and why of it. We are now and we will be forever. To confuse the comforts that illusions offer with living a meaningful existence is an unreasonable choice. There can be no purpose in living in illusions.

The Devil is only as powerful as the law of miracles allows. Control is nothing more than our own creation. Total control is the total absence of love. Our Creator is love. Love is perfection. Control is total chaos. Total control is the Devil. The devil lives in chaos.

These are choices we have the power to make that have irreversible cosmic consequences for the future of our species. Death is not an ending unless we choose it to be. Karma, as our species has incorrectly chosen to believe, does not exist. Karma could only be in a universe functioning through the use of control. There is only one of two outcomes for each of us when we complete our life. We either remain in creation or we surrender our souls, or our lives will be reassigned in creation at the cosmic level. There is no pain and suffering. There is no heaven or hell.

Once we have been created, we will always be in creation unless we choose not to be. If we make incorrect choices, we opt out of the creative processes; like all illusions, we cease to be once we become part of one. If we choose to fade away, it is a painless choice; to sleep and be no more. Death is an illusion supported with myths that can only exist in our denial. Nothing that is created under the laws of creation will ever cease to be. But all that is created out of nothing will never be or ever be.

Life is in the now, not tomorrow or sometime time in the future. With the illusions we now live in, there is no doubt that so many give up on life and die a thousand times before we fade away. All that does not remain in creation will fade away. All that has a purpose will return or remain in creation until that purpose has been served. To fail to accept that our life is not dependent on forms of matter is to fail to enter the path to perfection. Forms are dependent on matter. Life is dependent on nothing but acceptance and correct choices. Ensure your success in the now; accept perfection as your choice.

We have so much to understand. We have spent almost our entire existence attempting to live a lie. Now the lies are exposed. Lies are illusions and myths therefore have no basis in reality. We are who we choose to be. A lie is easy to define. A lie is any word or action with the intent to control. Now that lies are exposed for what they are, all lies can easily be determined. A lie is evil, an attempt to control. It cannot be a lie if there is no attempt to control. You will from now on know when you are being lied to; there will be an attempt to control embedded in the words. There will be no benefit to you if you are not given love and no control included in the help you receive. Control always comes with conditions which require each of us to give something in return. It is our very selves, our souls that always must give.

It is disconcerting we accept one lie as the truth because we do not know for sure that it is a lie. Then we refuse to believe a truth that we cannot prove either way. Death is a mystery because our Creator formed us to live forever. We decided that we must die. Buit where is the proof? There can be no success if we must sacrifice our individual beings with no chance of knowing our Creator as we were intended. Death is not our destiny. Our purpose is to maintain this earth as we know it. Death means no more than loss of purpose. Creation is based on purpose. Our purpose is to enhance creation. When we try to control, we are choosing an incorrect purpose. Those of us who seek no control are well on the way to finding success.

Choice is our all and everything. Our time here is limited, but if we choose, we will go home again and remain in creation until we attain perfection. A journey of wonder, peace, and brilliance.

Our understanding of the universe must include the acceptance of one Creator. Our place in creation has a purpose. Our Creator gave everything in creation a purpose. Only each of us must choose this purpose. It will never be forced on us to choose. But it must be our choice. Without a purpose we will no longer be a part of creative planning. You are safe to believe this: there are those of us who will live forever.

Death

We have chosen death as our faith. This is not a correct choice. The only correct choice is that we are forever, once we are created, a belief based on the laws of the universe.

The word *faith* is a control word. The word *belief* allows no control. These two words may be the basis of all the disagreements about the origins of everything. Those who choose evolution choose the word *faith*. Those who believe in creation choose the word *belief*. These two words correctly describe the difference between illusions and reality. Because of our gift of choice, we can choose to remove ourselves from our material bodies, but our souls live forever.

Life is both a gift and a challenge. Those who live their life for all it is worth and love life are rewarded as outlined in the law of miracles. Many lives; many miracles.

CHAPTER 12:

ENSURING YOUR SUCCESS

Nothing is certain. This is because of the design of our universe. But your success is guaranteed within your inborn potential. Your unique success is waiting to be attained; it is provided for in the law of miracles.

Timing is so important. In your journey to success, time is relative. You can begin anytime but the sooner the better. But once you make the choice to remain in creation and to never try to control, time will not matter. Your success will be attained at some place in time. Either in this form of your life and matter or in other forms up until you attain perfection.

The first step is to discover who you are. Then accept who you are now and determine who you want to become. Who you want to become is more challenging or less challenging because of where you are now. Once you overcome the fear and uncertainty of your now, everything will come together as you progress. We often believe success can only be attained at the expense of others. We also believe that we will be happy once we become successful. Both are the results of incorrect thinking because of the structure of creation. Success can never be attained at the expense of others because that success would only be an illusion because of the universal law of control. Happiness can only be attained once we attain perfection. Happiness is a shared experience. We can both give and receive happiness. Success comes from within us; happiness flows through all of us. But we can choose to reject both happiness and success. Our essence or souls, once created, remain a part of our Creator. Therefore, once we leave our earthly form, we return to our Creator. Once again, the parts return to the whole. Our Creator is the sum of creation.

Success is temporary. Happiness is forever. Our materialization was for the purpose that each of us would have the choice of becoming the unique spirit our Creator defined as our soul's meaning. We are here to experience our limited life, and we also have the choice to become more loving and higher beings. This alone should remove fear from your existence. Matter can be removed but it never goes away. It only changes forms. Your life never goes away, but it may fade away and then form again. Where there is life, matter is waiting to form once there is a purpose for that life.

There are two forms of our existence. One is the world we live in. This represents our daily existence, our environments, the physical earth we inhabit, and the bodies we now inhabit. The other is our spiritual existence. Our spiritual existence never changes. Our spiritual existence is life itself, our Creator. The last twenty thousand years must be undone. We must go back to who we were before we can return to our true meanings.

We are never too far from our Creator because we are part of our Creator. But we have the ability to remove our Creator from our souls through our choices. This means that we live in our own self-created reality. Our true reality comes from our very existence and flows outwardly through our hearts, our creation of a self that will determine our perfection. Success may be defined as living this life for all it is worth and then returning from whence we came.

Your life as you are formed now is only temporary. Therefore, your success is limited to your present entity. Your happiness is to be found in the acceptance of your purpose and in the attainment of your purpose. Once you determine your purpose, you will find a meaning for your entity. Once you have discovered your purpose and meaning, your success is guaranteed because of the law of miracles.

Once you have purpose and meaning in your life, nothing is impossible to overcome. The laws of your universe will become part of your essence once you make the choice to remain in creation and then never to seek control.

The choice to remain in creation is the greatest choice you will ever make. But when you do make this choice, it requires your lifetime of commitment. When you make this choice, you are making a promise to yourself that no matter what circumstances you find yourself in you will never waver. In essence, you are putting your existence under the laws of the universe. There is no more powerful way to live your present life form.

The choice to never seek control is the second most powerful choice you will ever make. This choice will enable you to live a stress-free existence. Choosing never to control may be at thought of at first as a sign of weakness. But in practice it is the exact opposite. This is because control is not included in the universal laws. This is our guarantee: once we choose to remain in creation and choose to never try to control, our success will be attained. We may never know where or when it will happen, but the where and when are sure to happen.

The law of miracles holds the universe together like a thread running through all creation. Design, control, limited expectations, limited choices, equity and justice, choice, prayers, and perfection are all included in this, the law of miracles. The sum of the laws of creation reveals the nature of our Creator. And so it is with your essence or soul; you are the sum of your choices.

If you have made the choice to remain in creation, together with the choice to never try to control, you are now able to access the benefits included in the law of miracles. There are unlimited benefits. Far more than we are able to understand, but nevertheless, these benefits will enhance yourself and guide your soul in its journey to perfection.

As you pursue your perfection, others will enter your reality to guide and aid you when you need them most. Embrace the universal law of miracles. The universe is a place of wonder. This is where our souls come from and the place where we will return. The time we spend living in our temporary place here is for the enhancement of our souls and the fulfillment of our purpose. The meaning of our existence will be revealed to each of us because the law of miracles surrounds and protect us. This guarantees us a choice in the now.

You are now operating at a higher level in your existence. Enjoy and embrace your temporary body. In time it will have attained its purpose and then change or decompose but always be ready to form once again. Your life will have a greater meaning, and you will have many more combinations with matter to touch and feel each of the higher levels of your creation before you attain perfection.

It is revealed that all creation is held together by forces we cannot understand. Through sounds and vibrations, these forces interact as if connected, much like permanent entanglement. The whole is the sum of the parts. Sounds and vibrations connect life and matter. It is the universal design. It is therefore your design. At the basis is the concept of self. This is the essence of you, your success in the now.

This is a new revelation. Our species is the first to have the choice to avoid extinction. All others before had no choice. We were given this choice to adapt to our environment and the awareness for our continued presence in creation. This is our purpose. We are even more important to creation than ourselves. But the connection is interwoven. This revelation warns us that we have only two real choices. We must enhance creation, or we will only choose to destroy ourselves.

How our species became so fragmented is a mystery. But the challenge for each of us is to remove controls from life, then to unite in our journey to perfection. In short, we are only created to maintain our universal selves. This will ensure our success because we will forever be a part of our Creator's plans.

CHAPTER 13:

REALITY IS NOT
A DREAM

The universe is real. Your life is not a dream. If life were just a dream there would be no choices. Live your life like the miracle it is. Dreams and illusions fade away in time, but reality is forever. You have the power to choose your life and reality, the greatest success system ever discovered. You will never need to seek another. This is your gift given to you at birth. Do you want to live an imaginary life without the chance to find your true happiness just because you are offered the illusion of something when there was nothing? These illusions are so easy to create because they are based on nothing. It takes no effort to create them.

Even though illusions are easy to create, they have no lasting power because of the universal truth stating something cannot be created out of nothing. All illusions and myths are nothing more than a denial of reality. Denial allows you to be controlled. Reality is accepting things as they are and making them work for you in your life. It is a humbling truth; you were not created to change or control the universe. But you were created to have complete control over your newly created soul. But this control is limited to you alone. Devote all your powers and go all out to understand this truth, because it will assure you that your singular place in creation is never-ending.

Nothing in this discussion of free choices is intended to, nor is it able to, detract from your life and your reality. The path you take in your life is your own choice. There are many of us who seem to accept this, but far too many refuse. The truth is constant, and your gift of choice is unfettered.

The notion or misconception that creation would be an improvement if it followed our designs is sour grapes and an unwise assumption. Our species does not have the intelligence or awareness level to design or create a universe of any kind or nature. In fact, we have yet to prove we can design and create our own selves. This is even though we have the awareness to do it and do it perfectly.

If life were just a dream, then nothing would really matter after all. It would be like waking from a dream and finding nothing. It could be that there would be nothing to wake up to or no experiences to remember.

The reality is that the universe, as designed by our Creator, may be unrecognizable to our species, given our propensity to live in illusions and myths. It stands to reason that in a simple universe, efficiently designed, we would find ourselves in a more pleasing place. An inherently more perfect place with all the elements of creation working in unison for the good of all creation and all living things; our Garden of Eden. Sometimes the truth is so easy to see, but denial for even a second in universal time can change your reality for all eternity.

We fear reality, so we choose to live in a dream like state. There is no fear in choosing reality. The real danger is choosing alternate realities. If we choose reality, all will be the same in all things that really matter. This will be our existence. There will no longer be too much of anything or the desire for more than needed. There will be balance and conservation of life and matter. Therefore, a successful life must be a balanced life.

We are in a false universe which serves the emptiness of modern humans, but nevertheless, it is not the universe we were created to live in. We can find our reality once again, a reality where everyone expects to take out for themselves as much as they put in, a universe with laws which are easily followed and binding, where everyone shares the results equally because no one expects something for nothing, a life we can make our dream—a reality-based dream. A life worth living. The greatest truth we must discover is that life is more than matter. Our bodies are composed of matter, but our life is composed of our Creator. Matter will always fade away once it has served its purpose. Life goes on forever.

But there is a disconnect between ancient humans, primitive humans, and modern humans. We all must reconcile our purpose. We must all survive together or only one of us can survive. As of now, primitive humans are in the best position to make the correct choices.

CHAPTER 14:

CONTROL AND PERFECTION

Each of us are unique in creation. We have no way of knowing where we are in the creative process or where we will be in the future of creation. The most important truth for us to accept is that it is our choice to remain in creation. We can choose not to be in creation, but we are created to be forever a part of the creative process.

Our God

Who is this God our species has created? We have taught our children that God created us in his image. Our belief is even more extensive, in that we believe God looks the same as we look. This elevation of our place in creation made us equal to our God. But then strange things began to come about. For confusing and mysterious reasons, we began to devaluate and weaken this God. This God became a mirror image of us, with all our faults and weaknesses. We have spent millions of years creating illusions and myths in order to deny our weaknesses by attributing them to be the weaknesses of our God. We say we worship this God. Could it be that in reality we are only worshiping ourselves? It is important to say it once again: our Creator is perfect. We have already been chosen. All that is blocking our path to perfection is CHOICE. We must freely choose. Are we the created or are we the creators?

The Creator

Who is this Creator our species cannot accept? Our Creator is perfect. In contrast we are not. Our Creator did not design us to be perfect when we were created. It would be our choice to make. Our Creator, being perfect, designed our creation to be perfect for all of us in due time. Creation is a process to be enjoyed, not a time or place. Within each of us is the power of the universe. Why do we continue to give this power to modern humans? There is but one Creator. There can be no success until we defeat control. The wisdom of our Creator is validated because our Creator knew that control was not possible in a universe composed with equity and justice as one of the laws of creation. Do you not see how impossible control is? Are you doing an excellent job of controlling yourself? Our Creator, being all wise, made control a nonfactor in a loving creation. Will we know how we are doing? The only known is that life will continue without our species or at a bare minimum, the final truth: only primitive humans will remain here on Earth.

Control

Control is deceiving, but in the end is evil. The truth is that control's only place in creation is to define perfection, therefore bringing into question the use of intelligence in the process of choices we make. We believe we have superior intelligence, but do our actions validate this belief? We adamantly proclaim that if our laws, rules, and regulations were to be removed, the result would be the total collapse of our society and creation as we have come to know it. This is sometimes called anarchy. The reality is that we are only a few more controls away from anarchy. A few more deceptions. Even after all these years, we refuse to accept the true nature of control and the only reason why control is part of creation. We cannot be both intelligent and wise, then believe in control as the basis of our creation. Control is our evil. Control ruins everything it comes in contact with.

We are, either by nature or conditioning, living under the illusion that we cannot take care of ourselves. This is not true. Once you allow control to be your protector or take care of you, you will become a servant of control. Our souls are ours to protect and maintain. There can be no freedom of our spirits until we take back control from other forces or beings.

Perfection

What is happiness? The answer is that happiness is bliss, a perfect feeling of perfection. Our Creator knows this to be true. Perfection is a progression ever outward until nothing remains but pure love. Such is creation. Creation is an expanding circle with no time restrictions. The processes of creation are ever-expanding levels of happiness until perfection is attained. The laws of creation ensure perfection. We can and must make laws, but only laws without any control. We must study the laws of creation and form our laws in the same manner.

Evil

Evil is part of the duality of creation. Evil is control.

Good

Good is not perfection. Good is the absence of control. The greater the love, the greater the good. Good forms the pathway to perfection.

The Struggle Between Good and Evil

Once our species was elevated to our new awareness level, our Creator opened access to love and perfection for us within our created limits. Good is defined as no control. Evil is control.

Good and Evil in Our Garden of Eden

It was approximately five thousand years ago that we began the fashioning of our God. The simplicity of creation was rejected and replaced with many deities among us. It could be that we got everything else right but our place in creation wrong. The flowers still bloom, the stars still sparkle in the night, beauty is everywhere, but happiness is not. Happiness and the simple joys of creation have been taken from us. The question remains why? Did we do this out of our own choices or were we forced or manipulated to obey? All the great thinkers of our time, almost as one voice, have concluded that without our control civilization will fall apart and that we will fall back in time and become subhuman.

The god we have created is a god of weakness. A god that would not be a god were it not for our control over all of creation. There are those among us or in control of us who want us to obey them and believe they control creation. They give us a universe and a version of creation that first compels us to accept their illusions and myths, then would have us believe that we are not entitled to any part of creation unless we lie, steal, or take it for ourselves by force. We may correctly call those doing this to us our Devil.

One theory may be correct: a culture with no interest in the laws of the universe or our Creator discovered our gift and our wisdom but did not have the awareness to understand our Creator and the laws of creation. This would explain why our species suddenly turned into an evil species around five thousand years ago. The belief that control is more powerful than love became our God.

Our Creator is not dependent on us for anything in creation. We were given our sacred selves with love and therefore no strings attached. All we have to do is choose and accept reality. Our Creator is perfect. Perfection needs no control. Everything depends on those of us remaining to choose the loving way of living within our own selves. Evil cannot exist if love is present. Evil is control. Love is perfection. We have the power to choose.

The belief that we can be successful in our newly-created universe is the end of our perfection in the now. This brings us face to face with this revelation: we may not be ready to raise our awareness level to the place needed to leave our primitive nature behind. We each must refuse to accept this newly created universe. If we do not, there will be no purpose, success, or happiness for those who refuse. Our existence is not lost or located somewhere in the future. It is in the now.

CHAPTER 15:
THERE IS NO CHANGING YOU

This concept is a reality and therefore you must understand and accept it. There are no judges, no juries, no inquisitions, and no human-made laws which can change or redesign you. We are each our own existence designed by a perfect intelligence which we are not granted, as of now, the awareness to understand. We control this: our limited life. There is no changing you because you are now part of the Creator's design.

To understand who you are you must first understand our Creator and the structure of creation. There are ten laws of creation. None are more important than the others because they together are the framework of reality. They are perfect laws. Together they form the basis of all creation. We cannot ignore them because we disagree with them or because we think we know a superior design. We have been trying to implement our own designs for over twenty thousand years or more and now just look at the results. We are now closer to chaos and annihilation than at any time in the last twenty thousand years.

Do we seriously want to take credit for where we are now? Are we really masters of the universe? Would our Creator and creation cease to be if we were to remove our control? This is the ultimate test of our reality, the false reality our illusions have created. We can be certain we were created with a purpose. Mistaking any species or outside forces as God's will, in the end, prevent our success in life. We are in a cosmic battle for our survival in creation. Reality is all around us but for unknown reasons we are now being prevented from understanding this truth. Your success depends on you understanding this truth and removing all control from your life.

At some point in time we must accept reality; why not now? If not for your happiness, why not for the happiness of those around you? You were not created to live outside the laws of creation. What is good for you must be good for all. This is but one of the laws of creation. Together all the laws of creation will change your life into a life of meaning and perfection.

The world is as it is, not as we wish it to be. For each of us, our world is as we choose it to be. Choice is real. Without choice the universe would become unsustainable, full of illusions and myths, therefore having no real meaning or reality.

You are the only you that you will ever be. You have control over your place in creation. But first you must choose to remain in reality. It is a simple choice, but because of thousands and millions of years of creating myths and illusions, our species seems to have lost the ability to see the nothingness of our illusions. The laws of creation are simple, but the complications we create when we continue trying to change them are far more devastating.

It seems the fear of reality makes us prisoners of our own myths and illusions. Could it be that we are a lost species, imprisoned by our choice to accept only the false realities which are our only means to save ourselves from insanity? Our species would be better served to return to where we were before modern humans or other unknown forces twisted reality. It may be that we are not ever going to access our new awareness. Not when we resort to primitive anger and violence to kill love before love can save us. We cannot be both an image of ourselves incarnated and, at the same time, be an image of our Creator.

What is progress for our species? Our progress has been slow, and when measured on the merits, the good is overshadowed by the not so good. We have changed the environment, but we have made practically no progress in enlightening ourselves. While our technology has grown by leaps and bounds, our primitive fears, instead of going away, have increased to ever-higher levels. Control is greater now than at any time in our short history here on Earth. We were not created to control. We were created to love and be the caretakers of this planet Earth, our Garden of Eden. In fact, we are now at the point where technology is going to completely control our species. We are truly making control our God.

Considering our short time on this planet, we have done more harm than good. We have created our own alternate universe which we have neither the awareness levels to sustain nor the creative powers to make a reality.

We have chosen an existence which may end up in our extinction. The question that needs to be answered is why we have accepted this existence when it has not worked for us over the last twenty thousand years and maybe well beyond this time. The truth is that we justify this existence because we do not choose to live in reality. The reality is that a few of our species are controlling us with illusions and limiting our lives. The question is, are the controllers part of our species or not?

All through our history, the masses have always been used for the benefits of those in control. But the answer is not control. If we choose to control, we will be no better than those in control now. The answer is not who is in control. The only answer that will work is that each of us stop trying to change who we are and therefore focus entirely on becoming the entity we were created to be.

Our fears are not becoming less; they are ever-increasing and being used to control us by using our emotions and perceptions to a greater extent than any time in our short history. Fear only distorts reality. If we are doing this to our own selves, then the end of our species as we now live, our existence, will be nothingness. We must choose to love or choose to control. Better to go back to who we were than to try and change our species into a new form of life that worships and thereby surrenders to control. We must not try to change ourselves or those around us. We must change nothing but our choices. Then all will be as planned.

Our Creator gave us the gift of choice. We have misunderstood the power of choice. We have used this gift to control. It is the same with creation. There is no changing creation. We must devote ourselves to understanding our unique selves and the laws of creation. There is no changing either us or creation. Why have we not accepted this reality over the millions of years of our experiences? It is precisely because we have created a god that is, in reality, our choice to be in control. We chose to abandon our Garden of Eden. We were not driven out; just allowed to choose to leave.

There is nothing incomplete in our species. Just as there is nothing incomplete in the laws of creation. Both were structured to eventually end our universe in a state of perfection. But this much is certain. Our species can change the most defective element in our creation: the desire to control. Everything we have discovered reflects the miracle and potential of our creation. Once we choose to let go of the fear of losing control, we will see that control is an illusion. We will be all that we were created to become; herein lies our success.

You were created with a unique essence. Therefore, no matter where you go, there you are. Just maybe it is better to be content to be who you are and where you are than moving around the world trying to change who you are. You can change your location but not your intended life your and purpose.

CHAPTER 16:
HOW IS YOUR LIFE NOW?

Becoming the best that you can be is your reason for living your life. It is all about the journey, the challenges you are overcoming each day, the obstacles that make you think. Your safety net is the two correct choices you are free to make.

They are: 1. To choose to remain in creation. 2. To never attempt to control. If you make these two simple choices, you will find yourself suddenly feeling content and unafraid. When you choose to remain in creation you will never cease to be. Removing fear from your daily life will be a blessing to you in itself.

So here you are in the now of your unique and one and only identity. You are you and there will never be another you. This is a miracle in itself, for you are the ultimate gift of love. Your universe is within you. You have total control of you. The gift of choice secures your life in creation. But where are you now?

Who were you when you saw the sun rise today? Did you wake up with no fears? Was your day filled with anger, guilt, and frustrations in your life? Did you feel that your life was something to be endured rather than be enjoyed? Did you have feelings of hopelessness? Do you feel controlled with no way out? This is not your reality. It is the illusion of control you live in. If you are one of far too many who currently have these fears and underlying feelings and perceptions, you can return to your reality. This will be your success.

The Way Your Life Began

In many respects, your life as you now know it to be began five thousand to two hundred thousand years ago. You are the product of thousands of years of control. The reasons why are not yet fully revealed.

From the time you could feel and perceive, you were conditioned to believe in illusions and myths. The first was the doctrine of original sin, stating that your ancestors were not worthy because God drove them from the Garden of Eden because they found a higher awareness. From that point on we were essentially removed from creation, being condemned to a life of suffering and pain. The implication being that God was intimidated by us because of our new level of awareness. This is our self-created illusion. As if this were not devastating enough, we were also faced with the threat of being condemned to hell, a place of fire and brimstone, if we did not accept the controls of others of our species or other forces and influences.

There are wars and threats of wars all around you. Fights between one center of population and another for no good reason other than domination and control. But why and to what end? There is the constant feeling of impending destruction of you and even this planet Earth.

Nations make weapons of annihilation and threaten to toss them about like rocks. If you turn on your television, this is the news you see: riots, killings, demonstrations, and politicians promising to give you something for nothing.

There are rules and regulations. So many that no one can follow or even understand them all. Yet we are content to vote for more laws and regulations under the illusion that we will benefit when all the laws needed for complete control are finally enacted. The question is, who is doing the voting for this? Certainly, it is not you. You see a world filled with hunger and starvation. Yet there are those among us claiming the majority of the wealth and benefits. The government sends checks out to many of your neighbors as payments for doing nothing. When anyone is paid to do nothing, it is slavery of the mind and spirit. Yet more checks are handed out, creating an ever-increasing number of those reduced to slavery of their minds and spirits.

You are surrounded by those who force you to give to them when it is of no benefit to you. Not only are you taxed at ever-increasing levels; you are forced to pay for tax collectors who charge you extra penalties for errors you did not intend to make. Taxes are charged on everything, and this is not enough, fees are added as extras you must pay for services you did not approve.

You are required to continually prove you exist by providing forms of identification, passwords, and codes. Yet you are allowed to vote for those in control with nothing but your signature.

You find yourself of no value to yourself. Your value belongs to others in control. Yet you are urged to believe that all is well. You are relentlessly warned that you would be in poverty if the government were not in control. You must never question all these never-ending laws and illusions. If you do, you will be become an adversary and penalized even more.

Progress is defined by imitation without validation. Everything is a copy, having no substance. All that is created are more illusions. We will become slaves to the controlled intelligence we are creating. Will we ever stop and think? Or will we become copies of reality and therefore copies of our species? Is this all there is? Could it be that we are copies of our own self-created realities?

This is where we are now. In danger of becoming a self-created species with no place to exist, except in our mirror of ourselves. In the now, this is where you find yourself. How is your life now?

The Way Your Life Should Be

From the time you could feel and perceive you were made to feel special. There are no wars or threats of wars. There is peace and tranquility everywhere. You were taught that you do not have control over anyone or anything other than yourself; that you were a unique creation. There is not another like you and there never will be. You were created with a purpose meant for you only. Your Creator designed it this way. Your life and place in creation is yours forever but only you can determine if you want to accept it or not to accept it.

There are no wars or rumors of wars. There are no fights between one population and the other because no one person or group desires any control over the other. There is peace and tranquility everywhere. Everyone understands that their awareness levels have not yet risen to the level needed to comprehend geometry, our first gift once we reached this new awareness we are now experiencing. There are no riots, killings, demonstrations, or kings and politicians. There is humility among everyone.

There are no rules and regulations. Our species is well on the way to becoming wise humans. There is no hunger and starvation, because no one has the desire to accumulate because there is no longer any need to control.

If your life began this way, you would fully understand that you are indeed in a Garden of Eden. This is all our species needs to know. Accept it, embrace it, because we are where we were created to be.

The reality of all of this is that our species would be better served just being ancient humans rather than living under illusions and myths. It is abundantly clear that our species is unable to adapt to modern humans or the unknown forces that control us. We are in our Garden of Eden; we need to refuse to follow those who want to force us out and reclaim who we are as a special species. If we are in our Garden of Eden, as all the facts indicate, then every minute we spend trying to find another location is time wasted. So throw away all the illusions and myths. Then and only then will you finally be able to see how your life is now.

CHAPTER 17:
THE LIMITS
OF LIFE CHOICES

The future is determined by the choices we make in the now. We created our past by the choices we made. To the extent that we made incorrect choices, we find ourselves out of harmony in creation as of now. Either we are in the creative process or now living in illusions which were our choices. It is true that each of us can begin making the correct choices now. All we need to do is begin, right in this instant in time. In the now. The more we stop trying to be in control, the more we will achieve satisfaction. Love and control cannot be moving in the same direction at the same time. The greater the love, the less the control. The greater the control, the less love. This is one dynamic of one law of creation, the law of miracles.

Our Creator created us with limitations on our ability to choose. We only have the ability to choose for ourselves. This means that when we attempt to choose for anyone other than ourselves, we are exceeding our ability to control. To control anyone other than our own selves is evil. To love anyone in addition to our own selves is good.

We will never fully understand creation until we accept the laws of creation. Our Creator defies explanation. There is only one Creator. Our species must choose to accept this truth or to become our own gods.

The limitations of life choices are in place now. In the journey to perfection, however, they will eventually become limitless until we are in a state of perfection.

Our universe is duality based. This is the reason why control is not effective. Control is one dimensional. At any rate we are not aware enough to control. We are under constant struggles to control ourselves. Our challenge is to continue to no longer seek control.

Understanding our place in creation must be our goal. There are limitations on our choices. Every time we attempt to control we drift into illusions. Happiness and success cannot be attained until we live within our limitations as we were created to experience.

CHAPTER 18:
HOW TO DESIGN YOUR SUCCESS

The universe is perfect because a perfect Creator designed it. Perfect yet simple. Limitless for all living things, yet subject to the laws of creation. These laws are exact and never will need changing but, for our species, these laws thus far seem too difficult to grasp. The great mystery is why. The answer is our choice; we do not choose to understand.

Our species, either through self-deception or other sources of control outside of our understanding, devotes our prayers to asking for things that do not add to our existence or we pray to satisfy our need for control. The reality is the only control we have is our ability to make choices. Therefore, prayers made asking for control are seeking things that cannot be or are not needed and will never be answered. An illusion is a false reality. Praying for control is a futile attempt to change reality. Yet prayers are a part of creation. But prayers are only beneficial if they are subject to the laws of creation. Not just one law: all laws of creation. The laws of creation form a perfect circle. If we stay in the circle of creation, we will always remain in creation. Creation is a perfect circle. This is all we need to know; in our access to success, all we need to accept.

Our Creator gave each of our species an existence like no other living things in creation. We are similar but no two are ever an exact duplication. This uniqueness is defined by the limited nature of our exclusive creation. This existence is commonly known as our entity or soul. Therefore, when we pray for anything outside our unique creation, they are no more than exercises in frustration. Yet we are taught the opposite. As a result, when we want something created, we pray for it.

One of the laws of creation is that our species cannot create something out of nothing. Yet we pray for money, expecting that our God will magically give money to us. This prayer is not reality-based because it requests something for nothing. At best it will be answered with an illusion. The illusion being that money is taken from someone else and given to you without any action on your part. This prayer can be answered only if you make the correct choice to earn the money yourself. If our species would only choose to live in reality and within the laws of creation, then the prayers we pray could be answered. Because we made the correct choices, we will receive the gift of becoming who we were meant to be. This will give us access to our success once we accept our place in creation and cease to expect something for nothing.

This is the beginning of the miracle in prayers. Think of it this way: when we wake up each day our only prayer needed is, "Show us the way to use all our life forces already in us to become the unique soul we were created to become." Try this and see for yourself. Only ask for what you already have in you to be the answer to your prayers. Your Creator will open your life forces and they will flow through your being. The result will be the creation of you, a special existence with the choice to remain in creation. This is all we need to know. There is no more than this. Anything more is an illusion that must be supported with myths and deceptions.

Make the correct choices to live within all of creation and you will have no stress or anger. Just give it all you have, and you will become the soul your Creator designed you to be. If we choose to accept the laws of creation, there will be prayers answered every day and indeed our lives can become a constant prayer. For those of us in creation who are in tune with our Creator, all our prayers are answered, no matter how long it may take.

The beginning of success in your life is to accept your Creator. We are not gods. When we create gods and lesser gods, we demean ourselves and lessen our understanding of our Creator. Then, also, we must stop praying for things we already have access to or that cannot be attained.

In the final analysis, the best prayer we can pray needs no words. We can make our life a prayer. How? By living with love and gratitude beginning now and forever. Every time you help someone with no strings attached you enhance your place in creation. Each time you help someone, no matter how you do it, you say a prayer for your success. These prayers are always answered.

Our Creator lives within us. There is no better way to assess our success than to open our minds to the power of self we have received from our Creator.

Success and happiness have been gradually taken away from each of us because we fear not being in control. We can put an end to this fear. There are two steps: accept our place in creation and never try to control others. Focus on you in everything you do. This is our guarantee.

CHAPTER 19:
ANCIENT WISDOM

Our species has twisted, inverted, and convoluted the laws of creation in order to prove that creation could be redesigned. The results have proven to be the exact opposite. The question remains, and as of yet is not answered: who and why? Who would do this to us? Why would we do this to our own species? If indeed we are doing this, then why do we do this to ourselves? Are we defective? Could it be that our species suffers because we are narcissistic? If so, who or what caused this mental condition in humans?

Modern humans have twisted and turned ancient wisdom upside down. They have given ancient wisdom new meanings just as they have done with words. Modern humans possess high levels of intelligence but little wisdom. They either refuse to accept universal laws or they intentionally distort them to create systems of control.

Examples of Corrupted Ancient Wisdom

Many Are Called but Few Are Chosen

The reality is that we all are chosen, but at this time very few know how to choose. We all are equal in the eyes of our Creator, subject only to the limitations of our own unique manifestations. We not can no change who we are no more than we can change the laws of creation. The real wisdom is that all are called (chosen) but only a few choose to make the choice..

Heaven Comes After Death

We are forced, trained, and taught through mind control to believe that Earth as we know it is a place of punishment. We have become prisoners of our creation. The result is that things we are asking for are unnecessary because we are looking for what we already have or were not created to experience. Our self-created version of Heaven is predicated on the illusion that our species can create, when in reality the only thing we can create is our self; this is because we have choice. Even our choices are limited by the laws of creation. The reality is that we are in Heaven now. So why seek more? Wanting more than creation can offer only opens the need for duplications and illusions. When we duplicate, we succeed in only making a copy. Copies are a false reality. Once each reality is experienced it becomes a part of our creative journey. As always, seeking to create a new experience above our limits to experience by using any form of control will only create a false reality.

Ancient wisdom is a corruption of reality with no basis but the need to control. Modern humans began the process of forming their own reality approximately twenty thousand years ago. This was the time when the Old Testament was written. The Old Testament separated humans from reality by creating a god in their image. Modern humans corrupted ancient wisdom to create the narrative that all rulers were divine and as a result infallible and exempt from the restrictions of reality. All indications are that this was deliberate.

Modern humans have continued over the past three thousand years to perform damage control. This is the time period when the New Testament was written. This was when the corruption of ancient wisdom went rampant.

Our current myths and illusions are the results of modern humans' continuing efforts to control. The signs are that modern humans are failing. Creation continues to advance. Good continues to advance. We have the choice to continue to advance. The conclusion being that our species cannot be removed from the creative process. The final choices have not yet been made.

The reality is that you can choose to remain you and you can remain in creation. Your success is the sum of your choices. Your success is in the now. This day, in this moment in time.

CHAPTER 20:

THE TEN LAWS
OF CREATION

THE LAW OF CREATOR DESIGN
THE LAW OF CONTROL
THE LAW OF LIMITED EXPECTATIONS
THE LAW OF LIMITED SELF-CHOICES
THE LAW OF EQUITY AND JUSTICE
THE LAW OF MIRACLES
THE LAW OF CHOICE
THE LAW OF INCORRECT CHOICES
THE LAW OF PRAYERS
THE LAW OF PERFECTION

These laws are not a menu; we cannot select only the laws we like. All choices we make that do not conform to all ten laws of creation will be incorrect choices. We must remain in the circle of creation. This is not that difficult to understand and accept once we accept our Creator's love.

The timeline was between five thousand one hundred to twenty thousand years ago; it was somewhere in this time when geometry and the laws of geometry were revealed to our species. The exact time is not that important. But there were seminal changes in our species. These changes are why we are where we are, in the now. Those of our species understanding these revelations were pushed aside or forced to submit to the control of modern humans during this time period in creation. The truths revealed in the ancient gift of geometry were lost in the illusions and resulting confusions. Modern humans rule through the use of control. They created the myth of the survival of the fittest; control became the path to their survival. Our world became a world of illusions. The laws of our species replaced the laws of creation. Creator Design became human design. Our species has been violating the law of Creator Design for thousands of years. As a result, time has stood still for us for all these thousands of years.

The Law of Creator Design

Creator Design is a perfect combination of all the laws of creation. This is the only universe that can exist. This is because our Creator is perfect. It does not matter if we are able to understand or accept it. What matters most is that we admit we cannot replace or improve it.

The fear of reality was used to control our species through the creation of myths and illusions. All is based on our fears of losing control. Control cannot replace choice. Control destroys all life. Complete control will destroy creation. Control exists because it is part of Creator Design. We are controlled only when we have no choices. We can make all the laws needed to maintain stability, but none can be sustainable if they contain any elements of control. Our Creator designed it this way.

Our Creator, under the Law of Creator Design, chose our species to receive the gift of choice. Because nothing was needed or expected in return, it was truly a gift of love. This gift is ours, always within our being, waiting to materialize; always waiting for us to choose or not to choose, thereby allowing us to be on the outside of creation throughout the creative process, thereby losing access to our souls. But we will be in creation—even if we do not know the how and why—forever.

The Law of Control

Our Creator possesses perfect knowledge and understanding. Control blocks out understanding and knowledge. This knowledge was given to our species the instant we were chosen. Our Creator knew this and therefore did not include control in the planning of perfection. Only as a means toward attaining perfection. Our species, with our designing of our own creation, got it exactly upside down. We believe, in our ignorance or because of our over inflated egos, that control is the pathway to perfection. We are created within our Creator's Design, but will we be wise enough or aware enough to accept that the only control we have is self-control?

The Law of Limited Expectations

There are limits to the creative process but not to perfection. When we expect more than reality, we break the universal law of limited expectations. This always leads to the creation of myths and illusions. Wanting more when there is no more takes away from the enjoyment of the present, the now in creation.

The Law of Limited Self-Choices

In creation there is contentment in knowing and accepting limitations. Wanting more than we can be takes away from the happiness and wonder of the now. The discontent we create within ourselves removes the experiences of our moment in our unique creation. Every instance when we want more than our limited creation gives us access to, we trigger the quick fix of control. The happiness and enjoyment of the creative process is and will continue to be accepting and following all the laws of creation. We have the awareness, but will we make the choice?

There is comfort and peace to be found in all the laws of creation. We definitely have limitations in our self-choices. Not understanding this law of creation is the cause of so much individual suffering and pain. Our Creator gave our species the best that we can be and feel, yet we have so far rejected it all. We continue to believe the fault is not in ourselves but in the nature of creation. There are those who believe that our species are the new creators and that our Creator has failed. Have we created the ultimate illusion?

The Law of Equity and Justice

We believe that our laws, rules, and regulations will at some point force everyone to become equal. But to what end? If you want to think clearly about this concept, change your perceptions. First remove denial from your life. Then observe everything that is going on in our world. There are so many laws, rules, and regulations that it is easier to break the law than it is to live within the law. The frightening trend is that more and more laws are being enacted, with each law intended to exercise more control than the laws just made. Why does no one have the wisdom or courage to question why the laws, rules, and regulations are not working? The belief is that at some point in time when all the laws, rules, and regulations that can be enacted are implemented, our species will dominate all creation. If we continue to accept our laws of illusions as a reality, we may find ourselves completely dominated, the exact opposite of what we need. Our species was created to be free. We can deny this reality, but we cannot change it.

The Law of Miracles

How would a perfect Creator design creation? The first consideration would be that nothing is certain, therefore there can be no control. Then there is the concept of the efficiency of creation. This means simply that nothing created ever is discarded or is destroyed. These concepts and considerations may or may not be within the ability of our species to understand or duplicate. Yet there are far too many of us who vehemently, and in some cases violently, dispute this.

Reality-based creation must be limited but limited only because reality is all there is. The goal of creation is the attainment of perfection. Life is unique unto itself. Matter is a means to an end. Life is best understood as a journey or process which ends in perfection. Matter is best understood as created to enable the attainment of perfection. Once perfection is attained, matter implodes because it is no longer needed. But matter cannot be destroyed; it can change forms to be used once again. This is the perfection of Creator Design. The universe has no meaning for each of us until we understand and fully accept the law of miracles. To really understand creation is to see miracles every day, all around us.

The Law of Choice

This may be true, but it is not a sure thing; everyone would choose perfection if given the choice. Choice determines our destiny. Do we fulfill our purpose for being here or do we choose to fade away? Life is in us. We must not choose to allow life to leave us. We were not created to remain here. It is our choice.

The Law of Incorrect Choices

How do we determine if we are making correct choices? For a choice to be a correct choice, it must contain one simple element: no control. So the first choice is to accept creation. All correct choices must begin this way. There is nothing going to keep you from making incorrect choices but the desire to be in control.

The Law of Prayers

There is always a path to perfection. The law of prayers provides constant access to perfection and our Creator. Prayers are silent communications with our Creator. Our spirit is in constant contact with our Creator

The Law of Perfection

Perfection is a place of no control. There is no something for nothing in the attainment of perfection.

CHAPTER 21:
THE MEANING OF LIFE

B efore we can determine the meaning of success, we must first discover the nature and meaning of life. The meaning of life will become incomprehensible if we do not first define the meaning of all creation. This seems unknowable at first thought. But it is not an enigma. This is because life is the same, but the meanings are defined by the purposes for that life. The meanings have everything to do with it. Reduced to the basic level of understanding, determining the purpose and the meaning of your life will follow. The tendency to overcomplicate reality is the cause of confusion and uncertainty.

The meaning of life for the entire universe is defined by its purpose. Existence with no purpose is meaningless. The meaning of each form of life may be for only one unique purpose and therefore limited. Therefore, there are limited expectations for that life.

Universal life is designed to enable energy and matter to expand to their maximum levels. The purpose is to experience happiness and fulfillment. Once perfection is attained, energy and matter will no longer be needed. Perfection will have been reached. After perfection there will need to be a higher purpose before energy and matter can emerge once again.

We are unique and yet at the same time part of all creation. We were created to love but our purpose is embedded in our newly created essence. We are here to learn through our own experiences. We are part of it all. In the end we will be where we choose to be. We are part of a universal consciousness. Our bodies are temporary but our souls, the essence of life, are forever. Our desire to control will go away once we accept and believe in a universe that always was and will always be in the now. This is to say that everything is in the now. We are part of our Creator. We must replace fear with acceptance, control with love. We are here to experience and to learn. We can choose how to live this life, but we cannot change the reasons for our being here.

The sun has a purpose. Even though it is not a living thing, the sun is composed of energy and matter. Even though it does not contain life, its purpose is to support life. Therefore, this is both the expectation of the sun and the limitation of the sun.

The universe is duality-based. The composition of life is not. Life is one-dimensional in that life is constant, but energy and matter are the variables.

Balance determines the purpose for energy and matter. Perfection determines the purpose of life. Everything in creation, to be effective and therefore remain in creation, must maintain balance. Once balance is lost there is no meaning in life, no purpose.

Life is what it is meant to be. Energy and matter are the emergence of balance in the now. Each has its own purpose. The difference being that life is permanent; energy and matter are only temporary; their purpose is to maintain balance.

The meaning of your success is determined by the meaning of your life. Therefore, your individual success is determined by the purpose of your life. Your purpose is to become you. This is the meaning of your success.

Think for a moment. Was our purpose as a species to change or redesign the universe? Where did this come from? We have been seeking control well before we became modern humans. Now this may be a weakness we may not be able to overcome. Our weakness prevents us from seeing our failure to control. We are wasting our time and place in creation when we become angry and lash out when we are confronted with this truth.

As always, before we question or deny we must first understand the meaning of life. We are here to prepare ourselves to become superior beings. Those of us that understand and accept this will become all that our Creator gives us the choice to become. Yes, our Creator gives us the choice to become all that we choose. Only limited by the universal laws of creation. Herein lies your guarantee of success and eternal happiness.

CHAPTER 22:

WE MAY NEVER MAKE CORRECT CHOICES

Why is it that our species may never make the correct choices? Our self-image may not allow us to be able to make correct choices. Even though we can clearly understand that our choices are incorrect, our self-perceptions are not clear enough for us to see the error of our ways, so we continue to make them. The laws of creation are binding, but because of free choice, our species is not compelled to accept them.

Another reason is because of our own fears, we are allowing others to control our choices. Doing this for thousands or millions of years, we have created a matrix that will require a dramatic change in our understanding of the power of choice if we are to return to our reality. The one thing you should keep in mind is that, regardless of how anyone other than you might choose, you can remove yourself from this matrix simply by choosing to remain in creation and then never again seek to control anyone but your own self. You cannot and should not ever seek to control anyone other than you. The laws of creation will not allow you to control others. Once you begin the process of controlling yourself, you will be the unique entity that the Creator granted you the choice to become. The refusal to live in reality comes with a price to pay. And this price is paid in the now.

Living a life of illusions and myths is easy. This is made easy because of denial. Denial is based upon the primitive fears of primitive humans. We are now at a higher awareness level. Our primitive fears are no longer effective in the process of our path to perfection. Now that we have choices, fear is very effective because it makes us easier to control. This is why there is so much fear among us. We have the new awareness level to make the choice not to fear. Our actions no longer need be predicated upon fear.

Modern humans have changed words into weapons of fear and, up to now, these words are very effective. You can free yourself from words of fear and control because you have the power. There are actions available that you can take to remove all fear from your life. Once you remove fear from your life, you will discover new revelations which will give you the freedoms you have never experienced up until now.

Our species continues to make incorrect choices. This process began when we attained our new awareness level. Because we are by nature a loving and caring species, most of us want to make the right choices. But unless we overcome the forces of control, the creative process will go on and we will fade away. Our species will become extinct. One thing is true: we are not in sync with the universe in this moment, our forever now.

The salient explanation for the reason our species is lost was the rejection of this place in time as being our Garden of Eden. This may have been the first denial. The very first attempt to control. One thing that is certain: this myth alone has changed our thoughts on life and reduced us to slaves to modern humans or other forms of control. As a species, if we are ever to take back our self-control, we must remove the primitive reaction of fear. Fear is no longer effective in the survival of our species.

Myths That Make Alternate Realities

There are several myths and illusions that are now supporting our human-made alternate realities. The first myth was that we were cast out from a magical garden because of our new awareness. The effect of this was the illusion that we obtained this awareness in defiance of our Creator, rather than it being a gift of love. The Devil was born when we chose this illusion of control. We created the myth of evil to justify our illusions of control. We personified this desire as the Devil. There is no evil or devils or demons except in our self-created myths. These personifications and myths are the blinders our species have chosen, to prevent reality from exposing our fragile egos. The only enemy of correct choices is control. The myth we have created to deny this truth is that control is an identity we call the Devil. There is but one Creator. No other gods, demigods, or entities exist in the Creator's universe. There is but one Devil and no other demons.

The second myth we created was that the Creator gave awareness to only a select few, then granted them the wisdom to rule over the rest of our species. The unintended result was that the more control they had over us, the more control they would take. There is no power in control, only the illusion of power. Control can never be more than a false reality, created under the illusion that an alternate or more efficient creation exists. There is a cosmic arrogance in our choice to create a more efficient and sustainable creation using our limited place in creation. It is as though if we all agree that we can change reality, then a new universe will magically appear. All we have done is to create an illusion. This is mind control. Our species is well beyond mind control if we only see ourselves as we now exist. But our own self-perception is flawed. Because for now our awareness is controlled by our refusal to see ourselves as we were created.

The third myth our new species created was that God first created us, then decided to condemn us as unworthy. This placed us at the lowest level of creation. We were in effect cast out of creation and punished, but why? We believe this on the one hand and then proclaim that we are the chosen ones. This is control-based, but who is doing the controlling? Is it our own species or unknown or more powerful forces? Why would we do this to ourselves? Could it be that we are delusional? How could we be both the reason for creation and the reason we were driven out of our garden, the very garden we were created to enjoy? This is insanity; an illusion lost in the flow of time, never having any hope of becoming reality. Believing that creation has many locations is just another illusion. We are in creation now and we will always be, in some form. To choose to believe otherwise is the creation of an illusion. We are in paradise now. Why let fear take it from us?

The fourth myth is that we must earn our place in creation by enduring pain, drudgery, and suffering, and then only by the sweat of our brows.

This myth controls our consciousness so much that all forms of slavery are accepted as normal, bondage, economic, class, and all other systems of control. No other living things are subject to this illusion. This is all the proof we should need to see, proving to us that this is one of the greatest illusions of them all. This is the creation of modern humans. But we support this illusion by creating other mythical gods and then attributing to these gods our own image. Yet our species refuses to reject these myths. Truly we have become what we have chosen to be. Just where do we think we are now?

The fifth myth is that only God's chosen few are gods, and they are to be worshipped by those they control and follow their laws without question. Thus, our species has created illusionary gods. Either all our myths must be true, or our species is heading toward oblivion. The end will come and thus all illusions will end.

The sixth myth is that our species can create something out of nothing. This myth, as is in all myths, requires the illusion that we can create our own reality through the use of controlling others. This law of creation is simple and easy to understand. Our species has the awareness level to understand and use this law in the now and thereby change all of humanity for the better. Universal law: something cannot be created from nothing.

The seventh myth is that our species can decide penalties for those who choose to make the incorrect choices. This myth exists because of the illusion that our species can create. We can in reality only create ourselves, but even then, only within the laws of our limited creation. In every instance when we make laws or employ rules, regulations, or any other forms of restraint, we only make matters worse. Control always creates illusions and supports myths.

The eighth myth is that the chosen few can make laws, determine crimes and punishments, and regulate all others of our species. Laws are illusions of control. We create lesser gods to rule over our daily existence. Do we not realize that this is not like our Creator? At the end of the day, we are only living in an illusion. The hopelessness, anger, and frustration we are experiencing is the result of making incorrect choices. Why do we choose to believe that we can improve creation by creating an alternate reality?

The ninth myth is that by allowing the chosen few to retain control of our species, the passing of time will eventually enable them to become the creators. There are no chosen few. We are all equal in creation. Each of us are a unique, never-before-formed entities. We will always be as we were created, provided we choose to remain in creation. The primitive reflex of fear continues to condemn humans to serfdom and servitude. If we make the correct choices to accept the laws of creation, we will no longer suffer the illusion of fear.

The tenth myth is that a loving God condemns our species to suffer and pay for our sins and transgressions until we are no longer in this life with little hope that we will be forgiven. Then to make it even more stressful, we may be cast into a mythical hell, filled with fire and brimstones. Where are the benefits of a life that is lived under such overhanging gloom and doom? The larger question is: who benefits? One certainty is that you do not. But then maybe the law of miracles allows this to happen for a reason, but only if we make the incorrect choices. The important truth for our species to know is that we have the power to make correct choices. Creation is designed by our Creator perfectly. We can only choose or not choose to participate.

Why do we choose illusions and myths? The Creator designed creation to be choice-based. The greater the awareness, the more choices that are created. The more basic the elements that are in the creative process, the less choice involved. The lesser the awareness, the lesser the choices. At the base level, the choice is to choose creation itself; this is a creation-based reality. It is clear that we are now experiencing a higher level of reality and awareness. The reasons why we are unable to understand or use our new awareness levels remains a mystery. This is our task, to remove the veil that limits our vision and clouds our self-realization. Happiness is the reality of now. Believing happiness can only be found in another place or time makes this time and place easy to deny.

The conclusion must be that we have the choice to make a life that our Creator designed or the choice not to. It is evident that our time here is not our all and everything. We must accept it and seek to live it rather than control or change it.

The reason we may never again make correct choices is that we choose to believe we are powerless. The authorities know this is their only hope: that we continue to believe this.

It is so easy to live an illusionary life. Most of us do not understand the power of choice given to each of us where our very existence can be realized. We feel powerless, so we wait for death, not knowing that we have made that incorrect choice. This is why we may never make correct choices.

CHAPTER 23:

CREATOR DESIGN

The Creator designed all life; therefore, you and each and every one of us. The Creator is love; therefore, we must love ourselves before we can become the image of our Creator. Then and only then can we remain in creation. Why? Because when we love, our control is limited to ourselves only, and there will be no desire to control anyone other than ourselves. Control is the opposite of love. When we try to control anyone other than ourselves, we become less like our Creator. Control is our own creation as the result of incorrect choices. So, we have created our own Devil. Our Creator, out of love, allows us to choose this Devil. This is all by Creator Design. If we love ourselves, then we will not need control, even of our own selves, but only to remain in creation. This means that we will be free of all controls in our life. Our Creator intended for us to rise above the need to control.

We must continually seek reality. Reality is far less complicated than the myths and illusions we now live in. Reality is based upon Creator Design. Think of it this way: all creation is like a river. Our Creator designed this river to flow forever without ever diverting from its intended course. We can choose to experience life in the now. Our universe is designed this way.

The Creator-designed reality is the only reality. In fact, the Creator-designed reality may be drastically different from the illusionary reality our species has created. Our species must accept this reality with all the limits it may impose. We may find a world that is drastically different from the illusionary one we now live in. We must prepare ourselves for a reality shock. Our egos may be too fragile to accept true reality. The true reality is that our species is a part of creation, not the reason for creation.

There would be no doctors, therefore no pills. No medical costs, because medicine as we know it would no longer exist. The quality of life would rise to the highest level in human history. This is because of one of the laws of creation: THE LAW OF EQUITY AND JUSTICE. Meaning, that which is not good for everyone cannot be good for just one only. We now measure quality of life by how long someone lives. It may be entirely different when Creator Design takes place. Our ideal life span may be much shorter. But the quality of life, happiness, and human progress will be at all-time highs and continue to go to even higher and higher levels.

Life is not defined by how long we live but instead on how long it takes to ascend to the next higher level of awareness. Science will be devoted to finding natural medications through the study of preventions and cures already in existence. The illusion of pills will be exposed as the illusion and myth that supported them: something for nothing. There will be no more controls; therefore, our creation will take less time to flow.

The human-created sciences and mathematics will no longer exist unless they are no longer used as a means of control. Our unique being is in no need of science and medicine unless there is no cost or control included. Creation is free. The answers are within us. All is free, so no control is a part of our existence.

Religion, as now practiced, is predicated upon worship. It is primitive to worship. In your journey to success, you will discover that all creation is based upon acceptance. We worship only that which we fear. To eliminate fear is to accept reality.

The illusions and myths that we have used to create our current economic system will cease to be, because they were created out of nothing. This will be almost impossible for us to accept because of our desire to control. No more taxes, corporations, currency, or any other forms of control; all will be replaced with non-control-based economic systems. There will be no controls, so everything will be accessible to all. This is our destiny if we choose it to be.

The illusion that we must pay for anything will be exposed. All the millions-of-years-old illusions were created because of our desire to control. Creator Design never allowed for this incorrect choice to last forever; only as long as needed to maintain balance. Currency must be based upon the law of equity and justice; therefore, nothing must be paid for; everything must be earned. Reality check: unless everyone is paid the same amount of pay, costs will never be more than mere illusions. Nothing can be paid for unless it costs the same for everyone. Remove cost and a noncontrolled currency will emerge. This is indeed a new revelation.

Creative design guarantees that we can attain perfection. We have the choice to accept it or to reject it. But we cannot change it.

Creator Design is the beginning and ending of creation. We are nowhere near the awareness levels needed to be able to understand it all. But we have the choice to continue to move toward that level.

Universal Laws Are in You

THE LAW OF CREATOR DESIGN: Our Creator is perfect. The law of Creator Design ensures no predetermined outcome. Choice determines everything. And so it is with our life. Choice determines the totality of you.

THE LAW OF CONTROL: This law ensures there will be no place in creation for control. All laws of creation are the sum of the total. They bind together like strings. They form an ever-expanding circle of perfection.

THE LAW OF LIMITED EXPECTATIONS: Reality is forever, so why do we expect more when we create myths and illusions? If you observe the sun when it rises every morning, it never changes. We can try to enhance the sun by using illusions and myths. We can call the sun a god or try to change it in any way, but we only create illusions. The sun, in reality, is there for us every day, to be enjoyed over and over. It is a mirror of the creative process. Reality is all there is. The laws of creation are all the laws there are. Our species has rejected these laws from the very beginning of our new awareness. As a result, many have been on hold in the creative process. Not all of us, but far too many. This is the reason we are suffering, even though we have all that we will ever need in our personal universes. Expecting more will only result in fear, frustrations, rage, and detachments, ending our attempts to succeed.

THE LAW OF LIMITED SELF-CHOICES: When we are created, we are one of a kind. But we are all the same as humans. Like the sun or a flower, we are a mirror of creation. Only our choices are limited because of our unique place in creation. As a part of creation, we will forever exist. Our place in creation, once we are created, is our choice.

THE LAW OF EQUITY AND JUSTICE: We are not created equal. We are all humans, but each with different souls or essences. Our limitations are inherent in our creation. We cannot change this law of creation. If something is not good for all, the law of equity and justice will not allow it to remain in the creative process.

THE LAW OF MIRACLES: Once again, our species must acknowledge that we cannot fully comprehend this law of Miracles. This law guarantees that our Creator will have the final choice over our place in creation. Under this law, once any living thing is created it will never cease to exist. It is not karma or reincarnation that we have created to give the unknowns meaning, it is more like another chance to return again because of our Creator's continuing design for each of us and our unique place in creation. We may reappear again at any time to complete or amend our design, or we may be assigned another place in creation in our journey to our perfection.

THE LAW OF CHOICE: This law is easy to understand. Choice is everything. Choice determines all outcomes. But our Creator has the final choice, as included in Creator Design.

THE LAW OF INCORRECT CHOICES: This law is central to the law of miracles. The continued use of making incorrect choices in our lives removes miracles when we need one the most.

THE LAW OF PRAYERS: Our species must relearn how to pray. Prayers are always needed. Once we combine all the laws of the universe in our daily prayers, they all will be answered.

THE LAW OF PERFECTION: Our Creator is perfection. Love is perfection. To the extent that we love, that is the measure of our perfection. The law of perfection does not allow something to be created out of or formed from nothing. Perfection is the highest love. There is no control once perfection is attained.

Creator Design ensures that all of creation will come together perfectly. Perfection and love are the same word. The same concept. What does this mean for our species? Simply this: we can choose to withdraw from reality, but we can in no way change reality. We were created and therefore we will remain in creation, under the law of miracles.

Death is an illusion created by our species. We created the myth of death out of the desire to control. We are here in our Garden of Eden. This is by Creator Design. We must accept the gift of love, choice.

CHAPTER 24:
THE LAWS OF SUCCESS ARE WITHIN YOU

There are so many reasons why we are where we are. One of the reasons is that, for over thousands and millions of years, each generation of our children have been bombarded with negative thoughts and lies and false reasoning. This is why we are confused about who we are. Our reality has been taken from us ever so slowly. We are living in a forced reality where there is no success because there is no awareness of self. The laws of success and the laws of creation are the same. Choose to accept either one of them, then you will automatically receive the other.

There are binding laws in creation. These laws are the same laws that are binding in your attainment of success. In the next few pages, several of them will be mentioned. They are all connected, however, and cannot be changed or made to stand alone. These laws are part of your being. They are within you, ready to be put into motion.

The universal law of equity and justice allows no choices to be valid which are not good for all life. Meaning that all the choices we make must be good for everyone, not just for the majority or a select minority. This law is not only efficient but is essential. In your discovery of your personal success, you must seek equity and justice as it forms your persona. Do not concern yourself with what is fair or not fair for others; only for you. Allow others to choose what is fair and just for their place in creation.

We were created with the awareness to experience perfect love. But we must make the first correct choice: to freely choose. This easy choice most of us seem unable to recognize and accept. We are allowed to make incorrect choices because our Creator, being all-knowing, included this within the laws of creation. Those of us who choose to make incorrect choices are thereby slowing down our time in creation and at the same time we are putting at risk our probabilities to remain in creation in the form and unique identities that we were intended to experience. Incorrect choices alter our places in the passage of time. The universe does not measure and evaluate time as we perceive time passing. In fact, time constraints are not part of the creative process because time is not subject to control. Your success will be measured by how much you have experienced love.

The most denied law of creation is that something can be made out of nothing. When we choose to believe that we can do this, we will find out that all we will be able to create are illusions. Once these illusions are created, if they are to last, they must continually be replaced with never-ending illusions and myths. Modern humans have been doing this over and over for thousands of years, believing these illusions to be real. This is nothing more than living in a state of denial. We are deceiving ourselves and refusing to face reality. All we have to do is look all around us, there is proof of this everywhere.

Those of us who choose not to live in these false realities are regarded as simpletons or out of touch with reality. This is a textbook example of attributing a defect we have and projecting it as a defect in others. This is often a component found in the illusion of elitism. Denial is always embedded in the illusion of control. Control is not included in the perfection of creation. Control is the basis of all forms of slavery, with economic slavery being one outstanding example. Something can never be made out of nothing. The circle always has a center. The circle cannot be broken. Everything emanates from the center. Reality is the center of the universe; you are your own universe. Reality is your perfection. Choose your perfection now. Your success is based upon your ability to assimilate the universe within you. The greater your effort, the greater your success.

The law of miracles is the perfect embodiment of creation. It contains all the wisdom of our Creator. It is the law that made perfect the formation of the universe. We may never fully comprehend how this law was designed, because it is so comprehensive that it is beyond our current level of awareness. Nevertheless, it ensures that we will find a place in creation once we make the choice to remain in the creative process.

The law of miracles makes it possible for the unexplainable to take place. This law allows reality to resurface once we reject the illusions of control. The law of miracles includes prayers. Once we understand this law of creation, our prayers will be answered. Prayers are a gift of love, because our Creator created us to experience love. This is the love our Creator freely gives, if only we would make the choice to accept our place in creation. When we pray, our prayers are answered with no strings attached. There is no need for offering gifts or making sacrifices because our Creator provided each of us with all we will ever need. All we need to do is accept our place in creation.

The prayer for understanding is the most answered under the law of miracles. This is because once we make the choice to understand the laws of creation, we will automatically obtain wisdom. We are either in creation or we become illusionary entities. Those of us who are unwise become victims of our own choices. Under the law of miracles our prayers for others are the first to be answered because they are prayers of love. Miracles are unlimited. Rebirth is but one miracle. We may not fully understand the law of miracles but when we accept this law, we will begin to experience love in the now and throughout all eternity.

Once we accept that we are not creators of any part of the universe other than our own existence in creation we will remain in creation forever. Miracles do happen and they occur every second in creation. Your success is your miracle waiting to happen. Your success is in itself a miracle. Look within you for inspiration. Some call it prayer, but no matter what we may name it, inspiration or self-knowledge, it is there, so look inward when you search for your success.

Modern humans make incorrect choices based on the illusion that we are intelligent enough to outthink and outsmart our Creator, but in the end the Creator will include those of us making incorrect choices in the processes for the advancement of our species to ever higher levels of awareness. This reality will become easy to understand once you read this entire book. Then freely choose to make the choice to accept this new revelation.

The universal law of miracles ensures for each of us our place in creation until our individual miracle occurs. This place in creation is a place in time when all living things are on hold, waiting for a transformation or opportunity to receive a new beginning. The Creator provides each of us with gifts of unlimited possibilities: a return to reality, a new awareness, and also to return to where we were, only more enriched in wisdom and enhanced awareness. This is our Creator's plan for each of us; when we choose to remain in creation against all attempts to force us to choose to reject creation and the Creator, this law of miracles ensures that we will remain secure in our life and our destiny. This is a truth; we are a part of universal design. We never need more than that which is in us. Accept your success for the miracle it is.

There are no exceptions; every living thing has the same gift: choice. Choice is ours as long as life, our Creator, flows through our existence. We cannot refuse to make at least one choice, because not making a choice is a choice; if we do, then this—the one and only choice we make—will be an incorrect one. We can choose to make incorrect choices. We also have the power to choose to make only incorrect choices. The correct choices will ensure we remain in creation. To remain in creation means that we will exist forever or until creation, through the law of miracles, finds a place for us. The quandary of our species is that we must choose the Creator's choice or choose the illusion of control. Will we make the correct choice of remaining in creation? The prospects are not promising as of now. Our species already has all we need provided for us in our Creator's design. Once we choose to accept this, our lives will be stress-free and filled with inner peace and ever-increasing levels of awareness in the expanding circle of creation.

There is no other meaning that we need to seek. The perfect prayer for understanding is all we need to pray for, and these prayers will always be answered. Then we will enter the never-ending flow of creation.

The meaning of all this for you should now be beginning to become clearer and clearer. But this is just the beginning.

Do we have choices or were we created to serve and support the choices of others? There are many questions, but we will be able to determine correct choices only if we understand the importance of choice in determining who we were, have become, and the reasons why. In order to comprehend choice, we must first grasp the design of the universe.

The formation and design of our universe were chosen by the Creator and therefore it was designed perfectly. This means that nothing will ever need amending and that the processes will never be subject to change or redesign or ever need to be adjusted. This never-changing design was the Creator's choice. We have the ability to make choices according to our awareness, but all our choices are subject to the limitations of our unique, individual purpose in creation. This is our reality. There are both correct choices and incorrect choices. This is the guarantee that we can choose a successful life, but only if we remove all fear and illusions when making choices. There is no upside in making incorrect choices. When we make incorrect choices, we become disconnected from the creative process. Incorrect choices create illusions and are destructive. At the very minimum they remove us from our own life, the life we have the potential to live.

From the time we make the first incorrect choice our lives begin to lose focus and meaning. This at first may seem confusing to you. But we are life, and our Creator is life. This means life and its Creator flows through us and is the same process in the creation of all living things. The sooner we begin to make correct choices, the faster we become ready for our next level of perfection. As our awareness levels increase, we will have more and more choices, but we must always be aware of this truth: our choices cannot change or enhance the laws of the Creator.

When our choices attempt to change or improve the laws of creation, they become myths or illusions. Correct choices are the steppingstones in the process of creation; incorrect choices remove us from our existence because choices are determining factors in creation. Intelligence alone cannot make choices correct; for a choice to be a correct choice, the entire force and laws of creation must be included. We will either understand and choose to accept this or choose to reject this and thereby end our participation in our unique existence in creation. Understanding this truth will make every choice we make an obvious choice in maintaining our life in creation.

When we are forced by any one person, group, or any other entities to make a choice, the choice we make will be of no benefit to us. Force is never a means of love or benevolence. It will always benefit the person, group, or entities forcing us to accept their choices or not allowing us to make a choice. The truth is that our Creator allows no one but each of us, our individual selves, to make choices for ourselves, unless we choose to allow others to make them for us. The reality is that we were created as unique and free spirits; therefore, all choices made for us by others cannot benefit us; they destroy our spirit.

The Creator included incorrect choices in the laws of creation; therefore, they are part of the creative process. To choose not to accept this truth is to accept myths and illusions. Our creation is not without limitations. Even if we do not make a choice, creation will go on. This is because choice is the catalyst of creation. Making no choice is a choice. Creation is not subject to our will or choices. If this were so, we would thereby become the creators. Our species cannot create so we regulate, the result being that we create our own universe of myths and illusions filled with our delusions of power, domination, and control but resulting in only the control of our own species. Our species is so obsessed with being in control that we are willing to deceive ourselves.

All choices made by us, or any living entity, made outside the Creator's laws will have the effect of limiting our life experiences. Incorrect choices are the only evil in our lives. We incarnate incorrect choices as evil and personify them as the Devil. These choices cannot be a reality in this universe, only in a false, meaningless alternate universe, filled with unlimited forms of mind control and gaslighting. Control is our self-created Devil. The Devil is a myth that supports the illusion of control. Control is an illusion in creation and creates all forms of denial.

The universal law of equity and justice allows no choice to be valid which is not good for all life, and also in compliance with the limitations of creation. Meaning that all choices we make must be correct choices, not the choices of the majority or a select minority. This concept is not only workable, but also unchangeable in the laws of creation. This means that all choices are either correct choices or incorrect ones, but there can be no merging, meaning that none are interchangeable. We were created with the option to freely choose to accept perfect love. There is no control in the laws of creation, and none needed in the perfection of the creative process. Perfect love allows no controls. We were created with the awareness levels needed to understand correct choices. But first we must make the first correct choice: to freely choose. This basic choice our species seems unable to recognize and accept. We are allowed to make incorrect choices because our Creator, being all-knowing, allowed them to be made within the laws of creation. Those who choose to make incorrect choices are inadvertently slowing down the creative process. Incorrect choices alter our concept of time. The universe does not measure time as our species measures time and records time. In fact, time constraints are not part of the creative process because of the nature of control.

Time: The Present, the Future, and the Now

Time is relative. Time is not a means of measurement. Time is only in the now. Time is the simple marker at any point from the beginning to end; the beginning of creation to now. This means that time has no purpose. Therefore, time does not exist. The beginning and the now are one and the same. This concept may be beyond our ability to comprehend. Think of it this way: if everything was created at once last week then they are both in the now. The concept of there being no beginning or ending seems a reality.

Violated Laws of Success

The most violated truth in the processes of creation is that something can be made out of nothing. When you choose to believe that you can do this, all you will be able to create is an illusion. Then, if this illusion is to last, you must replace it with additional illusions, limited only by the number of illusions you choose to make. Modern humans have been doing this for thousands of years, believing their illusions to be true, but this is a form of denial. We are deceiving ourselves and refusing to face reality. Just look around you, there are examples everywhere. Those who choose not to live in these false realities are singled out as simpletons or out of touch with reality, a textbook example of self-projection. Denial is always embedded in the illusion of control. Control cannot exist under the laws of creation. This law of creation, that something cannot be created out of nothing, is the most violated law in creation. It is the basis of all forms of slavery, with economic slavery being the outstanding example. Once any living thing chooses to live in this imagined reality, their existence is both over and forever removed from creation. Something can never come from nothing. The circle always has a center. All emanates from and is dependent upon the beginnings. The center of the universe is our Creator.

Our species at this time suffers from the failure to understand and accept the supreme laws of creation. Any choices or limitations imposed by any living thing must be for the benefit of all in creation. If it is not, then it is of no benefit, other than creating illusions. All illusions can only be made believable by creating myths and the greater number of illusions the more myths that are created. Not one illusion will last without myths to give it a foundation of denial.

Yet our species is constantly making incorrect choices. Are we wanting reality or will we gradually remove ourselves from creation by choosing to live in illusions and myths? It is our choice. But nevertheless, it is an incorrect choice. We must remove our primitive fear of losing control. Denial is a primitive reflex. It is of no use at our current awareness levels. We are now using it against our own selves or there are those among us using fear against our own species. This is unsustainable for our species. Because the Creator gave our species the gift of choice, we are able to make incorrect choices, incorrect laws, create illusions and myths, and incorrectly choose the illusion of control. Creation will continue. But those of us who make incorrect choices will not be in creation; only those of us who choose to make correct choices will remain. If we are so sure that we are so important in creation, we should be very concerned. It is indeed all for one and one for all. The dinosaurs, at their level of awareness, became extinct because they were subject to the laws of creation. Never believe that our species is an exception. There is no excuse for our species to make incorrect choices because of our greater awareness level.

The most misinterpreted law of creation is the law of miracles. The law of miracles includes prayers and is the matrix of creation. Miracles occur when we refuse to make incorrect choices because we remain in the right place and time for a miracle to occur. The continuous choice of saying, "I choose to remain in creation" becomes a prayer. The continuous choice of saying, "I choose to find a way" becomes the pathway to realizing your prayers.

You are a free spirit. Your entity is your limited universe. What better way to live your life than to incorporate these laws into your universal self? Success is simple if you want it that way. Illusions will show you unlimited ways to fail, but the simple laws of the universe will make you perfect in due time. Acceptance of the universe and who you are is the beginning of your success.

CHAPTER 25:
OUR REALITY OR OUR PERCEPTION

It is evident that an overwhelming number of us are living in a self-created reality. This in itself would be a pleasant experience, provided the incorrect choices of control were not included. In fact, it would be a healthy reality. This is because the laws of creation intended that all of us, because of our awareness level, can be creative and self-entertaining. It is only when we exclude any one or all of the laws of creation that we thereby remove ourselves from the creative process.

The high number of us making the incorrect choices are no more than empty souls that are in essence a waste of energy. This is the process that is necessary for the elevation of the next higher awareness levels for those of us freely choosing to remain in creation. The law of miracles allows nothing to be discarded once it is created. All illusions eventually go back into the place of nothingness from which they were created.

It is time to pause and think about the wonder of this all. A simple reality, one that we can all understand, because we are created with an awareness level that gives us the choice to understand and assimilate creation if we choose. It is indeed a stress-free reality. No religion, no fire and brimstones, no human rules, and controls. No fear, just the gentle breeze of the creative processes flowing through our minds once we make the never-ending simple correct choice to remain in creation.

The incorrect choice to attempt to live in illusions has opened the floodgates for charlatans. If you will allow yourself to see, just look: the tax collector creating more taxes and then using control to pay for more taxes created out of nothing. The makers of laws as a means of holding on to power and greater and greater control. Those in power create their own reality under the illusion of control. There are thousands more of every conceivable control manipulator on this earth right now. Reality will return them to the nothingness from which they were created, into lifeless energy waiting to return to creation once again.

All we see as value now will no longer have value because of the law of creation stating that something cannot be created out of nothing. While nothing will be free, everything will have value. This will mean there will no longer be starvation and poverty, because if there is something produced it will have value. We all see this in our life experiences. This is proof. Witness the man who has devoted his entire life to making more and more money. He never had a true moment of happiness. His satisfaction was creating illusions of power and control, only to cease to be when his existence is ended when he fades away, leaving behind lifeless matter. A life unused and therefore having no meaning; the decomposition of control.

We are so focused on sometime in the future that we have no perception of our now. If we continue to allow ourselves to be controlled, most of us will forfeit our happiness and success. The universal law of limited expectations is our key to happiness and success. Most of us do not spend enough time on living within the limited nature of creation. We continue to allow fear to rule our life and our perceptions. This is so tragic because control will go away when we no longer fear the loss of control.

CHAPTER 26:

THE LOST REALITY

I t is almost surreal, but there is a reality we all know to be true. I feel it deep in my spirit. I wonder if you do also. It is a memory of who we are or the reality of life; a life which was our existence far away in an ancient time, now a suppressed time. We all have within us the same genetic imprint that nothing can alter. We are in a suspension of time, far from the life we were designed to live. It was a sequestered life, but it was life itself. It was there for us to live with no strings attached. Then as time went by each day, this all was slowly taken away. First all life was the same for all of us, then over time it became restricted to everyone other than a select few; this has become our perception. Gradually we were somehow forced to forget our creation or forced into becoming a subservient species.

Then the illusions began, one after another. The supporting myths became our history and changed who we were meant to be. These illusions and myths were blended together, one supporting the other, until both became a more powerful one in blinding our perception of true reality. It is as if we became motionless, imprisoned in a time warp. Incapable of claiming our true selves because we have forgotten who we are.

This false reality emerged about twenty thousand years ago. It is telling that this was also when the first traces of modern humans began to emerge. There was enough for everyone. All each needed to do was to provide for themselves each day. Even with the unique life given to each of our species, we all were different, but there was no reason for one to be above the other. Everything was provided if we wanted it; all was there to gather or find. Enough for all within the laws of our creation. There were no controls. This was our garden to live in and maintain as our Creator designed it to be. All was well. The air was pure, and the land was fertile. Our Creator raised our species awareness level above all others and formed this earthly domain for us to protect and enjoy.

Our first incorrect choice was to separate ourselves into segments and class levels. This in itself violated the universal law of equity and justice. As a result, those with greater intelligence than all others assumed control. But intelligence alone is not useful in creation unless it is used without control. There is conclusive evidence that intelligence in itself can be devastating if combined with control. In fact, the use of intelligence with control as a component is the reason for the accelerating deterioration of modern humans. Even good intentions can have unintended results when included under the illusions of control.

Our Creator did not grant a greater awareness level to more than one of our species. This is why control will not change creation. This is why mobs, governments, ruling classes, and even well-intended control movements are doomed to fail. But the unintended consequences are potential eliminators of our species in the ever-upward flow of creation. Dividing us into classes was for one reason only; this was control. The ruler became the divine one, the top of the class structure. Then next were the priests and the overseers. The remainder were the lower class, the workers, and producers. Even though this was the producing class, they had no access to the wealth they produced. Thus they became a slave class. They were expendable and were subject to increased control.

It was during this time that modern humans discovered that matter could be used to create illusions. But once again the laws of creation would not provide for matter to be manipulated for control. Our species can manipulate matter, but only the Creator has the ability to change the form of matter. Every time our species manipulates matter it is either abandoned, deteriorates, or it leads to devastation or contamination.

The choice to create a king or a leader was natural. But making a ruler a god was a denial of our Creator. Yet this is what we chose to do. The lower classes were used as slave labor and became increasingly restless. Needless to say, they became increasingly difficult to manipulate and control. At first the illusion created was that a god chose the king to rule. Those who gave the king all the wealth in the kingdom would be the most favored in the eyes of the king-god. The upper classes were rewarded with power and adornments for serving the king. Money was created as payment for the working classes. Wealth accumulated into the chambers of the king. The value of money was a perfect illusion. The kings and all of their lesser gods made sure this illusion was never-ending by all the myths created to sustain this illusion of control.

In the choice to make laws, each choice included controls. Controls require illusions and myths to implement. Once the lower classes became discontented and turned on their own kind, those in control created laws. These laws were severe for the lower classes but not applied to the higher classes.

The choice to create money was the beginning of the concept of serfdom, leading to the concept of slavery of all kinds, all hidden under thousands of illusions and myths.

The choice to create a nation became inevitable because the greater the wealth the king accumulated, the more workers were needed. The king knew that the more workers needed, the more difficult it would be to control the ever-greater number of them. Creating a nation with boundaries provided the king with a means to accumulate even greater wealth. Keeping the working class placated required even greater illusions of money. The working class controlled the money; the king controlled the wealth.

The choice to create an army became the next illusion. This united the workers and deceived them into believing they were saving their nation when in reality it was the king and his wealth that was saved and protected.

The choice to create an army and go to war served the king and controlled the working classes even more. The illusions of honor attributed to killing other working classes in other nations began and created a killing spree like no other. It was after this that our species entered a place of madness and terror, all justified by our self-reflecting illusion that this was the way our Creator designed our species.

The choice to create wealth out of nothing was the next big illusion. It is important to understand this: an illusion is no more than a lie supported by myths which are lies told in story form. The attempt to create something out of nothing was inevitable. It is the only way that modern humans are able to maintain all their illusions. This is because our species cannot create reality. Our only choice is to accept reality. Do we have the intelligence to understand our new levels of awareness? We must rid ourselves of our primitive natures. Those of us who do will be in creation forever. Those who are not willing to choose the laws of creation cannot remain in creation. This is the truth.

The choice of illusions was the genesis of control. Remember, illusions are lies and myths. That which is created out of nothing will never last. From illusions, alternate realities are created, and to nothing they will return.

Here we are. We are kind, loving, and want no control over anyone. But this is where we find ourselves in this moment in creation. The good news is that we have choices even in this alternate reality. We can choose to remain in creation. We can also choose to never seek to control. We cannot change all the illusions that modern humans have created or the myths they have created to hold us in fear and bondage, but we can ensure our place in creation by making these two simple choices: to remain in creation and never attempt to control anyone other than ourselves.

Each time we rely on anger as a response we become animals once again. Remove control and we will become the entities our Creator reserved for each of us.

CHAPTER 27:

A PERFECT CREATOR

Attempting to describe or understand a perfect Creator is a challenge for our species. Nevertheless, the truth is that our Creator is perfect, and reality is the result of our Creator's choices.

This is an illuminating question for our species: for reasons unknown, there suddenly appeared on this page a onetime offer. As part of this remarkable offer, you had one minute to decide to choose yes or no. It is an uncomplicated offer. It states as follows: you have the next sixty seconds to accept or reject. If you choose to accept, you will live the maximum life you were created to live and your purpose in life will be achieved. If you choose yes, you will be given all you need to be happy, satisfied, and stress-free. This offer is simple and easy to understand. You must agree to accept creation and the laws of creation as chosen by your Creator. If you choose not, you have the choice to live your life as it is now because you see no reason to change. This is all you need to do: just say yes, I choose.

What would be your choice? (___) YES (____) NO The most crucial consideration in your answer would be the time element. You would only have a minute to choose. So, your minute is over, what was your choice?

Incorrect choices are not devastating unless the time to change them has expired. Once your time is over and you have not achieved your purpose, your body will fade away and your life will be returned to the creative process. A perfect Creator would know this. Therefore, no time limits would be included in any of the laws of creation. Therefore, everything created would be timeless in creation. Creation is no more than a process.

Time is no more than the measurement of the journey to perfection. Time is nothing but a perception. Time remains constant in reality or in illusions.

The answer you chose above is more about you than about creation or reality. Do you want to be controlled or do you want to be in control? If your choice was yes, it is evident that you do not want to be controlled. If your choice was no, then you want to be controlled.

Telling yourself that you want to be in control in order to serve others is not true. The only reason you would choose to be in control is to have others serve you or take what you have not earned.

There is a danger for our species. It is not because of creation, our Creator, or the laws of creation. It is our self-created universe of illusions. We choose to control every time we are given the choice. We must change this choice.

When we decided that we were the reason for creation, we diminished our perfect Creator.

The result often is when we diminish or reject our Creator we reject our ourselves.

We must stop trying to define and replace our Creator. Instead, we must accept that we are not gods. We are humans. We are part of a shared experience. If we continue to choose alternate realities, we may no longer have a purpose for existing. The solution is that we must restrict our purpose to live in the now. We must seek no control. Our efforts must be redirected to understanding creation, not trying to design it. We have a perfect Creator.

CHAPTER 28:
CHOICE

The law of choice is one of the ten laws of creation. No one law of creation stands alone. Together they form the circle of creation. If nothing else, this book clearly and with the utmost simplicity outlines the nature and power of choices. We make life complicated. As a result, we fail to experience life as it is designed for each of us. Wanting more when there is no more leads to boredom and frustrations, therefore a waste of your time and effort. All experiences are limited for each of us. These experiences can occur over and over and be enjoyed even more each time they occur once we limit our expectations.

Wanting to experience more than your creation allows will only result in magical thoughts and lead to the incorrect choices of myths and illusions. We must accept the reality that choice is a gift of love. The less we try to control, the more we will accumulate. Control is a limiting force in the creative process. Control in any form is evil. The universe is designed this way: the more we love, the less control is needed. Control can only exist in a universe that allows for something for nothing.

We believe our misleading thoughts come from the Devil. The reality is that all thoughts are part of creation. They are allowed to flow through our minds because of the duality of creation. Our Creator designed it this way because without this miracle of creation, we would not possess the gift of choice. No thought can be a part of our actions until we choose to think about it. Choice comes before action not after. The Devil is a myth. Incorrect choices enable the Devil to have a larger place in illusions and myths. The only control we have is over our own actions. We cannot control the thoughts of others. This is why when we try, we become more like the Devil.

Choice requires a higher level of awareness than our primitive ancestors had attained. For whatever reason, our species suddenly attained our current level of awareness. The very moment when this awareness began or how it began is unknown. But we can relax about the how and why because it is all by our Creator's design. Nothing can alter the creative circle because it is our Creator's Design. See in your mind all the laws of creation together forming a circle which binds them together with the Creator's design in the center. This is a perfect universe, and we are part of a perfect creation. This circle is the sum of its parts. As it is with the universe it is with you. Your success is the sum of your choices.

Why is the law of choice so important? Because in the end of it is all we have: choice. Our Creator intended it to be this way. So, the next time you hear someone say, "I had no choice," let them know that choice is all they have—and all they need, for that matter. It is the same for you or me. Choice is all we have. Our Creator designed it this way. Now all our fears are removed because, no matter what is going on all around us or no matter the circumstances, we, you, and I, will be untouched if we choose to accept and practice the laws of creation. Nothing else is required, nothing else is needed. You and you alone control you. Just as you cannot control anyone other than yourself, no one can control you. This revelation of new knowledge reduces your life to just a matter of choice. You are ready now to set yourself free.

Choice Is Not a Religion

Choice is a plan for life. There is nothing mystical about it. This book is all about choice. Once you have read and follow the laws of creation, you will never have to search for a self-help book again. These are simple laws which are easy to follow unless you are looking for more complicated and controlling ways to live your life, resulting in a mystical outcome, ending in nothing.

The error is that religion has been used as a means of control not teaching and understanding.

Religion Is Our Mirror

We have become a reflection of ourselves. We cannot take our eyes off ourselves long enough to become nothing more than illusions in time. We were created to love, first ourselves then all those around us. Accepting and loving ourselves is not selfish. We have the choice to worship ourselves, but when we do, we will no longer be capable of loving others. We must never choose to worship images. This is because our souls are within us and therefore our success comes not from without but from within. We can create our own images. Worshiping is to submit to control. This is because when we do, we submit our souls to the desires of others. No one who loves you will ever want you to submit to their desires: only to share them.

CHAPTER 29:
HOW TO SURVIVE LIVING IN ILLUSIONS

You cannot change creation. We are able to change ourselves only. This is to say that we have the ability to control ourselves only, but within our purpose for living. This is so easy to understand yet our species continues to deny this limitation. This is our place in the universe. We are not created with the ability to change or control others or the laws of creation. Those of us who cannot attain this awareness level will not remain in the creative process.

We cannot change the illusions and myths which surround us and distort reality. But we have the choice not to accept them. Meaning that we may use them to our advantage, but we must not ever make the incorrect choice of accepting their controls. The two basic means of remaining in creation are first making the choice to remain in creation and then to never seek to control. If we do this, nothing can deny us our place in creation or remove us from the creative process. These are the two simple, yet most powerful choices we can make.

We cannot live in creation until we relinquish the desire to control. Our Creator understood that the creative processes would be unworkable if control were needed. If nothing else, our species has proven our Creator's perfection. Just analyze the thousands of years we have been attempting to create anything through the use of control. What do you think? Have we created anything? Or was it all created before we distorted it all?

Even though illusions are not reality, they are lies well-told and concealed in false faiths and perceptions. You have control of all your thoughts and choices. You have total control of you, but that is where your control ends. So yes, you can make the choice to accept and live in illusions or choose to ignore or not accept them. You have the choice to accept whatever the results of illusions may give you and use them in an alternate reality-based place in your life. Illusions can only exist in a something-for-nothing universe. So never expect to gain when you accept something for nothing.

How to Change Your Life and Become the Real You

There are ten steps to becoming the success and the real you.

#1 DESIGN Understanding your universe is the first step. Each day is twenty-four hours. The universe was designed this way, and your unique universe is the same: one day, the universal now. Time is relative. Time does not slow down for you, but your time is never wasted unless you choose to waste it. Each day is a series of choices. Some simple, some complex. You have total control of your time but are limited to the structure of your own small universe, designed perfectly for you. Each day is your opportunity to create you and your unique life. Never become concerned about the passage of time. Instead focus on becoming the perfect you. This is your destiny once you choose it to be. The universe is timeless for a reason.

Once you are up and about in the morning, you decide who you will be that day and who you will become. The past may or may not have been your choice, but today you are free to choose. Tomorrow you will be the result of the sum of the choices made today; we are always living in the now. The time you used making incorrect choices is lost time. The correct choices will always shorten the time it takes to become all you were created to be. It is so important to keep in mind that you have the gift of choice, together with the awareness to choose wisely. This truth should be exciting to know and make your day one of wonder and ever-increasing expectations.

You have been given the ability to design your day any way you choose. If you want to do nothing, you can choose to stay in bed or just sit and think. Your day is yours to design. Your life is yours to create. You have the awareness to see your past choices and the wisdom to change them. You can ask yourself why you are the way you are now. Then choose to eliminate the choices that resulted in the you that you have become now.

If you allow yourself to study and copy the design of the universe, you will know how to design your life as it was intended. Those who are happy and successful use this design to make their goals a reality. This truth is very important in your life: you have only a limited amount of time to become all you want to be. Taking the time to think and plan will make you better than most. This is because so many never understand this reality. They go through each day with no understanding of who they are or who they want to become. They allow the limited hours of each day to be used for the benefit of outside controls, all the while expecting something to magically happen that will suddenly make things right and add some manner of meaning to their existence. If you submit to controls, you will be forced to become a meaningless person, both to yourself and to those you know.

Control is not included in the design of the universe and in the creative process. Control limits or takes away all choices. Remove control from your day and you will open the door to unlimited choices in your life. Choice makes your day and your existence one of unlimited outcomes.

There are unlimited accomplishments available to you once you eliminate control from your life. This is a case in point. You are at work and having a productive day. You are working and all is going smoothly. Then out of nowhere you receive a call from a high-ranking executive. He goes into a tirade, yelling without allowing a word from you. Finally, the conversation is over. But your day is ruined, and you are emotionally deflated. If you really understand the design of all creation, here is the way you choose to understand the reality of the phone call. He was having a bad day. You cannot control him or his day. So, you stop thinking about it. Simply put it out of your thought processes. His day is out of your control. Next go over the entire phone rant, then think over everything in the conversation that you cannot control. Let go of these things and remove them from your thoughts.

Now you are left with only the things you can control. These things are all that matters. You will see that all these things which you can control apply to you only. Now go over each thing and decide how you will choose to react. You can choose to find a new job or stay. If you decide to stay, then your choices are clear. Begin changing the things you can. Make the choice to become an even better producer than you already are. Do this with every thought about the phone call. The end result is that you are not controlled. You are now in a better place in your life.

Never try to use control or react to control. Always ignore control. Control is an illusion. Reason destroys illusions. Trying to change the reality of the phone call will only create false illusions, resulting in anger, hopelessness, and a feeling of disconnection in your existence. Control reactions, such as abruptly walking out and leaving in the moment, are an attempt to control the situation. This is like fighting control with control and this will not work in a universe that was never designed this way.

It is too bad for us in the now that so many have wasted so much time on trying to redesign our realities. What if we had spent the last twenty thousand years devoted to the understanding of the design of creation? Then too, what if you devoted the remainder of your life to that same understanding of the design of your existence?

All other things being equal, you can aways ensure your success by maximizing your day by avoiding wasted time and focus.

#2 CONTROL Knowing the limitations of control is the beginning of wisdom and happiness. A life devoted to changing creation is a life lost in the quest to control. Can you control the hours of a day? The answer is that the design of a day was created long ago. Many have tried, but time cannot be altered. You can choose to stay up with no sleep all day and all night, but you will only become isolated from your true meaning. The end result will be that you are too stressed out and exhausted to enjoy your life. You will have lost time and the enjoyment of reality, but nothing will be changed.

Attempting to control all things that you cannot control is the basis of all your pain, suffering, rage, and all of the loss of meaning in your life. Learn from your Creator. Stop trying to control realities and circumstances, and your day will be yours to design in ways you never imagined possible. Replace control with choice. You can control your thoughts, but you cannot control how others think.

Our Creator removed control as a means to obtain an end because to control everything is to create nothing. Your life design is a copy of Creator Design. So, if you control everything in your life you experience nothing. Replace trying to control with choices. If you want to eliminate sugar in your diet, instead of attempting to stop the production of sugar, choose to eliminate it from your diet. One is trying to control; the other is choice. It is as simple as it appears to be. Eliminate control with choice. You will be an instant winner every time.

The belief that you can change you by changing those around you is the exact illusion you are now living in. You are your reality. Changing the reality of those around you is the essence of evil that always results from control. Think of it this way: if you want something, choose a path to obtain it. Do not expect others to do it for you. Because if they do, they will become your servants under your control: you will become their master.

Illusions, by their very nature, always turn reality upside down. They provide short-term denials over long-term consequences. Control is the easy choice because it is an expectation that you need to do nothing, and all will be taken care of. This is an illusion. All illusions are not reality based. No one is created to serve you. Then too, you do not have the power to choose the existence of anything other than yourself. This is not a riddle our species must solve. It is a reality we must accept. The only way others can control you is to take away your choices. They cannot do this if you refuse to choose to live in their illusions of control. It is an illusion that you must serve those who control you, even if they live in their own illusions that when they are controlling you, they are serving you, when in reality you are their servants.

#3 LIMITED EXPECTATIONS There is a connection between limited expectations and experiencing a satisfying and stress-free existence. Reality is constant and never changes. Because of the gift of choice, we can change our reality but when we do, we are living in an illusion. This is our choice, but once we attempt to change the reality of creation or the realities of those around us, we become controllers. Then there is the potential for self-destruction and the destruction of those all around us.

Self-creation is our gift. It is reality-based. It is not selfishness to want the happiness and peace you were created to experience. Your life will become ego driven and selfish once you attempt to control others around you. Seeking to accumulate more than needed exceeds limited expectations included in the laws of creation. If you want to really enjoy your existence and be all you can be, focus on the things you know you can attain. Become your unique self, one expectation at a time. Constantly increasing your expectations without attaining the current ones will open the doors to wasted time and effort. If you do this you will not need illusions in your life. Illusions enable avoidance and takes away your reality.

This is a profound thought about expectations. One true muse contains so much wisdom. Why do so many choose evil? It is simple: because evil pays but good does not. An intelligent and self-aware species could solve this muse for the illusion it is. Stop paying for anything evil. This is the essence of all creation and the laws of creation. Why not? And why not now?

#4 LIMITED CHOICES You can never choose more than reality. The universe is created efficiently. Correct choices open the universe to you without constant setbacks and detours. Incorrect choices open up an alternate universe to you, filled with setbacks, constant detours, frustrations, and loss of self. After all is said and done, after your life has been lived, you cannot go back and change it. When you separate reality from all the noises and distractions, you will discover that the combination of limited expectations and unlimited correct choices were the best decisions that you could ever have made. All other actions would not matter because they were your illusion. Illusions take away from your time and place in creation.

#5 EQUITY AND JUSTICE The universe is equal in one respect only for our species; we all have choices. Without choices there can be no equity and justice. Once we form the habit of making the correct choices, nothing can take away our access to equity and justice. This is according to the design of creation. There are no laws in creation validating the accumulation of wealth, the domination of one over another, controlling others, or the consideration of self at the expense or detriment of others. When we measure our enjoyment and progress or place in our existence, it is all about our choices, only our life matters. Matter does not matter. So why measure the value of you, or anything in creation, based upon the accumulation of matter? Equity and justice are not found in domination or accumulation; they are found in living your life according to your choices and never trying to control anyone or any part of creation other than your place in creation.

#6 MIRACLES Understanding your existence is beyond your awareness level. The place of our species has yet to be determined to be a permanent process in creation. It could be that we are merely a brief sidetrack in the Creator's Design. Our species has substituted our laws of illusions to replace the laws of creation. This one incorrect choice excludes most of us from receiving or being included in future miracles in our existence.

#7 CHOICE From the very beginning, the gift of choice has been hidden by our ancestors. As a result, we live in a universe of illusions which we have come to accept as choices.

#8 INCORRECT CHOICES Just because we can make an incorrect choice is no justification for making an incorrect one. Once you take this route, one incorrect choice creates the need for another.

#9 PRAYERS In our world of illusions, prayers are most often used as a means of control. Knowing the power of prayers in a universe without controls will make living your life an exciting adventure filled with wonder.

#10 PERFECTION We must choose perfection or, if we choose the rejection of this law of creation, we will create an emptiness in our souls which we cannot endure. All the laws of creation must be a part of the journey to perfection and become one before perfection can be experienced. It must be earned.

CHAPTER 30:

REVELATIONS
AND MYTHS

The Perfect Car

A good parable of how modern humans have chosen not to face reality is this one. It is as if we were given a new car to drive, with no costs or strings attached. All we need to do is insert the key and follow the simple instructions provided. If we choose to do this, we will possess the only car we will ever need, and it will never need to be replaced or repaired. But rather than accept this car, we have decided to make our own car because we believe we can make a better one. It is apparent from the very beginning that we do not have the ability to do this or even to make a duplicate of this car. Then, for unknown reasons, we decide that we will pretend the car we have made is going to be better than the one we refused to accept.

Our false belief is that all we need to do is keep changing the designs and continue to replace or repair this same car, then with enough time, our car will be superior to the one we placed in storage. During this process we will have lost time and the enjoyment of the perfect car we refused to use in the beginning. In the end we have no reliable transportation. The perfect car for our needs is in storage while we deny it is there. For all our efforts we have been unable to manufacture a car that will not, at some point in time, fall apart unless we continue to make more versions with new shapes and model names. We do the same as the car owners in the story above when we create illusions to try and explain or justify our denial of reality. The car story is in so many dimensions a replica of our brief history.

The Story of Job

The book of Job is the only narrative in the Bible in which there is a conversation between God and the Devil. It is an unsuccessful attempt to explain why there is evil in the creative process. I am referencing it here only because it is the only entry in the Bible which validates the universal law of miracles. Our species must understand this law of creation (the law of miracles) because when we make the correct choice to remain in creation, no matter what the obstacles or illusions and myths may be, our entire being will remain forever in creation, even under the most impossible to overcome circumstances.

The law of miracles is our guarantee that we will remain in creation and progress upward to our intended perfection. This law of creation is the reason evil is a part of the creation process. This is because the proper identification of evil is a part of the purification and perfection of our species.

The book of Job is in all Bibles. It is a book found in the Ketuvim writings section of the Hebrew Bible, located in the Old Testament. It is a religious story that attempts to explain why the Creator allows evil. The universal law of miracles ensures that each of us will remain in creation once we make the correct choice to accept its perfection.

In this cautionary tale, the Devil challenges the Creator, saying that he can deceive our species and persuade us to reject the Creator by taking away our correct choices through the creation of illusions in order to confuse us. The Creator allows the Devil to deceive Job by taking away correct choices using myths and illusions. But in this story, Job refuses to choose to reject the Creator. Because Job refused to make this incorrect choice, he remained in creation. The Devil could only attempt to control the choices of Job with the hope that Job would make the incorrect choice to live in an illusion. Job would not. The Creator used the Devil to enhance Job's place in creation.

Below is a simple analysis:

Control (The Devil) challenges the Creator's laws. Control (The Devil), by creating an illusion, attempts to force us to believe we have no choices, so why believe in the Creator? We refuse to choose to deny our Creator. We continue to choose to believe in our Creator. Control (The Devil) is then unable to create a myth. So, the illusion cannot last. This is when the miracle occurs. Miracles are the universal rewards granted to all of us who choose to remain in creation, regardless of perceptions and illusionary realities. This is the universal law of miracles.

This was also the first story in the Bible revealing the gift of choice. Job refused to accept control. Job took all the power away from, and thereby destroyed, the Devil when he made the choice not to be controlled.

This story, in so many, ways reflects the temporary myths and illusions we all can choose to live in. But just like Job, we can choose reality. In the end we will return to our intended place, our special place in creation. The story of Job is the first example of the dividing line between the Old Testament and the New Testament. The Devil created the illusion that Job was being punished, but in the end Job was restored to reality. This was because Job refused to deny creation and chose to accept his place in creation no matter the consequences. This is an example for us. This was a miracle. The revelation of our universe is all around us. It is within each of us. Yours is ready. Just choose acceptance.

When Money Became an Illusion

This phenomenon began in the early 1940s. Money transformed from being a medium of exchange into a means of control. This was in violation of the universal law that something cannot be made out of nothing. Once the illusion that value could be maintained without an increase in what money could buy was established, the law that something cannot be created from nothing was set aside in order to placate the workers and protect the rulers. The average hourly rate was just under fifty cents an hour. The cost of a gallon of gas for a car was under twenty cents a gallon. A house could be bought for less than six thousand dollars.

But there was one factor no one noticed: even though wages continued to increase, the value of what the increased wages could buy did not. Value became an illusion. The cost of gas continued to increase, but the amount of gas money could buy went down. Mathematics became a nonfactor in reality. Currency became a perception. The cost of living went up in reality, but the buying power of money did not. The government began to print money based on no valuations but perception. As a result, having more money available began to have no relationship to valuations. We accepted this illusion without question and began to spend money without any restraints. There was nowhere we could not go and nothing we could not buy. The internet and the technical progress resulting in the invention of television reinforced all these new uses of money. We were happy in the illusion that we were in control, when in reality we were losing control.

As the number of illusions of control continued to increase we slowly began to feel that we actually had no control. Everything was ours to purchase but at a cost to our freedom of self. This was because our Creator gave us control over our own selves and nothing more. Once this was taken from us, we became entities without our sacred souls. All of the ever-increasing illusions removed us from our true lives that we were created to live. This is why our species now finds ourselves in a world we cannot cope with.

Wages then were fifty cents an hour. Now wages are over twenty dollars an hour. But the purchasing power of wages have decreased. Gas was twenty cents a gallon. Now a gallon of gas is almost four dollars a gallon. A home could be bought for about six thousand dollars then. Now a home cannot be bought for less than three hundred thousand dollars.

Think about the frail reality we have now created. We live in fear. Violence and killings are the norm rather than the exception. Government is the new religion. This has all come about because we are now being controlled. We have lost ourselves in this process. Our true spirits have been taken from us. Take this thought with you: control is a choice. Control is evil. Do you want to choose evil?

If you want to see in real time just how fast one illusion must be created to support another, how about taking a look at money and currency. It is the same for government, taxes, and the government payrolls. The law that something cannot be created from nothing is now replaced with an alternate universe with increasingly less and less meaning.

This story is based upon real events. We mistakenly believe that our place in creation is ever-expanding. The reality is that only our illusions are expanding at a malignant pace, resulting in a continuing eroding of balance in our lives. It may well be that our creation of an illusionary currency is the core reason why our economic system is not equitable.

Another Place, Another Time

In the beginning there was but one. There was no control, because in the beginning this was the perfect one. We identify this perfect one to be our Creator. We have gotten this wrong. Our Creator is in us, not somewhere in an imaginary place. Life is constant and forever. All other aspects of creation are variables due to the duality of creation. This Creator has no gender as we know it, just perfection with no needs; a feeling of fulfillment and peace we know as love. Wisdom and perfection are more than intelligence. This Creator created our universe and a universe that enables us to experience perfection over and over again with no limits. This universe does not exist outside us. It can only be found within each of us. This universe is composed of purpose, meaning, design, learning, experience, and fun. It is forever, meaning there is no ending.

This is our narrative. We create it. Our experiences become part of creation. We decide our purpose, meaning, and design. Why would we want more? It is not another place in time. It is in the now.

The time and place are not important. But the experiences are. We all are part of the Creator. Thus, our experiences will forever be ours to remember.

CHAPTER 31:
HOW TO GUARANTEE YOUR SUCCESS

Making anything complicated increases the chances that it will become an impossibility. Success follows the same pattern. Complications use up more time and energy, then often render less than the desired outcome due to poor use of time.

Ten Pathways to Your Success

33. Design
This is the most important part of your success. You can begin this process at any point in your life. The earlier the better. Believe it or not, you do have the ability to design your life and therefore your success. Most do not know this because we are encouraged to allow circumstances and others around us to decide who we are and how we live our lives.

34. Control
The basic ingredient in your success plan is self-control. You have the first and last say before you deviate from your goals. Begin at the lowest levels, then move up as you master each goal. You must maintain your vigilance and always keep in mind that your control is limited to your own self. Every time you deviate and try to control anyone or any circumstances beyond your universe, you will lose focus and place your success in jeopardy.

35. Limited Expectations
Knowing your limits and limitations eliminates frustrations and clearly defines your progress.

36. Limited Choices
There are only twenty-four hours in a day. If you are to be exceptional, use time as your life's currency. Spend it for maximum returns.

37. Equity and Justice
Not only expect the best, always push to maintain the next best level. Keep your vision on the way you must perform to progress. Balance everything you do. Balance is the path in the attainment of your success. Balance is everything. This is your belief in who you are and will maintain both equity and justice in your existence. Do not be concerned about the fairness or the unjust circumstances of the moment. Your success is not dependent upon fairness or justice; only on you.

38. Miracles
Throw blame and excuses out. Reject these thoughts. You make the choices. There is no magic. Your miracles are in you. Success comes with persistence. Miracles are the result of persistence and belief in your purpose. Miracles are the results of our Creator's infinite intelligence. We do not have to duplicate it or add to it: just accept it.

39. Choice
Most obstacles are in your mind. Constantly remind yourself of who you are and who you want to become. Then choose accordingly. Making incorrect choices may seem easy at the time, but they will limit your success.

40. Incorrect Choices
Incorrect choices undermine your success. Time will not wait for you to choose success.

41. Prayers

Some may call it prayers and others may call it meditation. But everything emanates from inside out, not outside in. Prayers are nothing more than communications with your Creator. Your Creator is in you and part of your purpose. The shortest distance to any point is a straight line. So it is with your conversations with your Creator. Prayers based upon beliefs will be answered.

42. Perfection

Success is putting all the universe inside you toward becoming your unique success. Put together an all-out effort. There is nothing without effort. No something for nothing. Rise above your perceived obstacles. Your perfection is dependent upon nothing but your choices. Success is following your heart to your purpose.

Why This Success System Never Fails

This success system never fails because it is not a one-size-fits-all approach. It is infallible because it is designed to adapt to you and your unique success. It is not based upon belief, only acceptance. The laws of your success are the same laws that form the universe. The universe operates under the same laws as yours with one exception: you control yours. Just do not think you can control any other universe except yours.

In our individual universes there is only one success for each of us. It has very little to do with fame and fortune or accumulation of matter. It is the perfection of self. Success may be defined as the attainment of happiness and protection of our unique souls or entities.

In our search for meaning, we must first seek understanding. Before the attempt to understand must come acceptance, the accepting of limitations. We are humans therefore this is our limitation. Our success may be defined as remaining human yet become more like our Creator each time we make the correct choices.

It all seems so simple. We believe that if we control everything around us, then we will be free. The simple truth is that until we master control of ourselves there will be no satisfaction within our souls, the essence of our creation. There is only one control that ensures your success: self-control. Begin today, in this moment in time, practice controlling yourself. There is a significant difference between self-control and being selfish. When you give of yourself freely with love and with no need for control of others, you are truly living a happy life. When we think we are helping others by controlling them we are in reality making others serve us.

Success is a way of life. It is the totality of your existence living within the laws of the universe. It is so true that the best things in your life are free. Your life is yours for living. You have no debt to repay or stand in line. Your life is right before you and you can begin living it now. This is your success, just accept it all.

CHAPTER 32:
UNDERSTANDING IT ALL

N othing has changed for me, you might say. This belief or current form of fatalistic optimism will, if not changed, destroy our species. The tragedy for us is that we may be content to enjoy the temporary optimism of illusions. Such is the price we pay for our gift of choice.

The question may be asked: why does a book about success require a new assessment of the universe? This is because success, as we have perceived it to be, is almost impossible to attain. We must first return to our reality or our success will forever be an illusion. We are spiritual beings. Therefore, success is the attainment of spiritual perfection. Accumulation of things: power and wealth signify nothing, certainly not happiness. Success is the experiencing of love, family, and finding your purpose. We were created to experience. Our happiness is dependent upon becoming the soul we were given the choice to accept.

Time

There are many concepts of time. It is believed that time stretches over millions or even billions of years. But time for us actually began when we were created. In reality time does not matter because time is not defined by anything other than purpose. So, it might be said that time is the line between the beginning and the attainment of purpose. The universe is timeless. It always was and always will be. For each of us our time is limited only by our purpose.

What Went Wrong

The only reasonable conclusion is that our species bears the blame. Our purpose was to maintain this earth and at the same time participate in all its wonders. We were in a state of perfection. How much time is remaining for us to attain our purpose? In the event that we no longer have a purpose we will cease to be. Wars are our only purpose, it seems. Control and domination of the many by the few is our chosen reality. If our purpose is to terminate each other our time will expire soon.

Our Choice

It might be concluded that we have so far failed in achieving our purpose. This brings up the very real chance that our place in creation may be lost. Our Creator does not create through the use of force or controls. We were created in our Creator's image. Our Creator chose it to be this way. Yet we choose force and control.

Our Place in Creation

In the end our place in creation is our choice. So, we may continue to live in this garden we know as Earth and enjoy our time here. This is our purpose. When we choose not, we may no longer have a purpose.

Animals or Humans

Our purpose was to become like our Creator and thus share in our Creator's experiences. We are in the Garden of Eden now. This is our place in our forever. There is peace and contentment here. We can choose to remain animals or become like our Creator and experience life as our Creator designed us to experience it.

Two Simple Choices

We have been given the gift of choices. Even if we do not comprehend the powers we have been given, we must not give them up easily. The first simple choice is to remain in our Garden of Eden. The second simple choice is to not attempt to control. If we do this we will remain in Eden.

Now

In the universe there is no past time. No future time. It always was and always will be. So, there is no actual time, only purpose. To think of time as a reality is to believe in control. We are all in a state of being. As long as we have a purpose we will continue to be. The purpose of creation was to experience. Therefore, creation will always be.

Balance

The universe is duality created. Therefore, balance is essential. There can be no purpose or meaning without balance. The use of matter beyond its availability will in itself remove balance from our earth.

Form, Energy, and Matter

Our universe is created through the combination of form, energy, and matter. Life is not the subject of any of these constraints. Life is our Creator. This is the reason you or I cannot create. Life is our Creator. There is no life in form, energy, and matter.

There are two forms of our existence. One is the world we live in. This represents our daily existence. Our environments. The physical earth we inhabit. The bodies we live in. The other is our spiritual existence. Our spiritual existence never changes. Our spiritual existence is life itself, our

Creator. The last twenty thousand years must be reversed. We must go back to who we were before we can return to our true meanings.

Experiences

We are most like our Creator when we desire to share the experiences of others. We love most when we do this expecting nothing in return. There is nothing so perfect as male and female in the experiencing of love. The creation of male and female could only be designed by an all knowing and perfect Creator. We are most happy and successful when there is love in our lives.

Anger

Beware of your feelings of anger. Anger results from the fear of loss of control. It is the difference between humans and animals. Anger separates us from our Creator. Our Creator could never be angry. Our Creator only creates with love.

Acceptance

One of the laws of creation is the law of limited expectations. This law is vital to your success. Our refusal to accept the limitations of creation is the reason why our species is in danger of becoming extinct. It need not be that way for you though. Those of our species refusing to accept the limitations of our creation will eventually destroy themselves. We can choose not to be in this group.

Purpose

Without purpose there can be no meaning.

Accumulation

Accumulation is now our barometer of success. The universe was not designed to allow for accumulation. In fact, accumulation always results in control. When there is too much accumulation, balance is destroyed. Once balance is destroyed reality can no longer exist. It may be concluded that balance is the pathway for attainment of your creation and thereby your success.

Revelation

Our purpose was to become the first living creations given the awareness and the choice to adapt. Before our creation all living things either adapted or did not continue to exist in the same form. We were given the gift of choice. Therefore, we can choose to be eternal. This awareness was the next step in the progression of our species.

Selfishness

In our search for meaning, nothing is more important than understanding just what selfishness really is. The perfection of self is not selfishness. We are constantly persuaded to believe that we have no purpose other than to serve others. To attempt to control others is the definition of selfishness. We all must accept that when each of us begin serving each other rather than controlling each other, then and only then will selfishness be replaced with love. This is the result of the law of equity and justice.

Modern Myths

Modern myths are now known as conspiracy theories. We should consider all unknowns with the same logic. Myths and illusions are no more than theories, yet they are accepted for the truth. This is because we do not choose to employ the same rationale to myths and illusions.

We must reevaluate all we know. Everything must be questioned. We are at a turning point in our creation. Nothing is going to be the same as we have been taught to believe. We must replace faith with belief. It is now more important than ever that we seek our Creator. Be careful when you feel anger, hate, and before you make the incorrect choice to kill. Love is perfection. Our Creator is perfect.

Putting It All Together

Everything must be understood in its totality. There is wisdom in balance. So it is with these thoughts and revelations. The sum is not greater than its parts. But the totality forms your reality.

We have never considered a universe from any other perspective other than our own. Due to our, as of yet, primitive fears, we are not able or willing to consider a universe without control. We view randomness as proof that a Creator does not exist. Even with the passage of over twenty thousand years we are not yet able to see that control is not possible in a perfect universe. In essence all we have is the now. Now is the streaming of our past together with our choices of today. This is our now. The only changes that are effective must be made today. In the now.

Special Offer for Those Who Purchased This Book

I believe that somehow, some way, our species will endure. We are just a few simple choices away. It is because of this belief that I am making everyone who owns this book a special offer:

YOUR NAME _____

ADDRESS_____
ZIP _____

DATE _____/_____/_____
DATE PURCHASED _____/_____/_____

AMOUNT PAID _____.___

Once this book sells 8,000 copies, for all books over 8,000, the profits will be placed in a trust or a reserve account. Every thirteen months the profits from all the books sold above 8,000 will be placed in the trust account. Every thirteen months each book owner will be paid an amount determined by taking the books they own times the average profits on each book sold.

Example: books sold 30,000 - 8000 = 24,000

Profits = $5.00 x 24,000 = $24,000 in profit account.

Total books sold 24,000 over 8,000 divided by $6,000 = your share for each book you own.

Books you own: 2 x $4.00. Total $8,00 If you own 10 x $4.00 . Total $40,00.

As the total book sales increase, so will your profits, based upon the formula above. We will all share equally from the profits as the law of equity and justice provides for in the universal laws of creation, specifically the universal law of equity and justice.

This is your universal certificate of ownership. To claim your ownership profits you must keep this book in your possession at all times. Once you want to claim your profits, present this as your proof of ownership. Keep this book and claim your profits annually. The same book can be claimed over and over until all profits are paid. To claim your profits, you must provide direct deposit information and proof of book ownership each time you submit a claim. If there is no direct deposit information, may be a fee charged to mail out checks.

ABOUT THE AUTHOR

BERNIE HESTER JR.
NOW RETIRED

INDEX

Milton Keynes UK
Ingram Content Group UK Ltd.
UKHW050658280324
440307UK00012B/456